SUPERQUAKE!

SUPERQUAKE!

Why Earthquakes Occur and When the Big One Will Hit Southern California

DAVID RITCHIE

CROWN PUBLISHERS, INC.
NEW YORK

To David Kogut

So many persons helped with the making of this book that it would be impossible to list them all here. They include my literary agent, Carol Mann; Jake Goldberg of Crown Publishers; Allan Frank, who provided many of the illustrations; Dr. Raymond Sullivan of San Francisco State University; and the librarians at George Washington University, Catholic University of America, the Library of Congress, and the Pratt Library in Baltimore.

Special, posthumous thanks must go to Tim Moore, who helped with research for the first chapter, and Thom Willenbecher, whose moral support was appreciated. They both took a keen interest in this project, but unfortunately neither of them lived to see it completed.

Published by Crown Publishers, Inc., 225 Park Avenue South, New York, New York 10003 and represented in Canada by the Canadian MANDA Group

CROWN is a trademark of Crown Publishers, Inc.

Manufactured in the United States of America

Library of Congress Cataloging-in-Publication Data

Ritchie, David, 1952 Sept. 18–

Superquake! : why earthquakes occur and when the big one will hit southern California.

Bibliography: p. 173
Includes index.
1. Earthquakes—California—Los Angeles Region—Popular works.
2. Earthquakes—Popular works. I. Title.
QE535.2.U6R58 1987   551.2′2   87-8877
ISBN 0-517-56699-0
10 9 8 7 6 5 4 3 2 1
First Edition

Contents

1

California: The Earthquake State

Someday in the not-too-distant future, much of greater Los Angeles will be destroyed. One of America's largest and most important cities will be shaken to ruins. Thousands of Angelenos will be killed immediately; many more will die in the days that follow, of injuries sustained in, or of various hazards caused by, the earthquake. The toll in human suffering will be tremendous. The economic effects of the disaster will rock the entire nation and probably other countries as well. This castastrophe has been virtually preordained by the forces of nature and the works of humans, and nothing can be done to stop it. To put it briefly, Los Angeles has been built to be destroyed, and its destruction—if present forecasts are correct —cannot be long in coming.

What you have just read is not alarmist rhetoric. It is the conclusion of seismologists (geologists specializing in the study of earthquakes) who have studied California's potential for devastating earthquakes and have judged that a large part of California, particularly its southern urban corridor, is ripe for destruction by a major earth tremor in the near future. In a 1980 report commissioned by then President Jimmy Carter, the Federal Emergency Management Agency described the danger facing Californians in the following sober words:

> Earth scientists unanimously agree on the inevitability of major earthquakes in California. Along the southern San Andreas Fault, some thirty miles from Los Angeles . . . geologists estimate that the probability for a recurrence of a similar earthquake is currently as large as 2 to 5 percent per year and greater than 50 percent in the next thirty years.

The report adds that "other faults [are] capable of generating major earthquakes in . . . the immediate Los Angeles region," as well as in the San Francisco Bay area and San Diego. According to the federal study, "the aggregate probability for a catastrophic earthquake in the whole of California in the next three decades is well in excess of 50 percent."

Translated into simple language, these cautious words mean that a major metropolitan area in California faces destruction within a short time. This disaster may befall any of several major cities along the California coast, but for reasons we will see later, the odds favor greater Los Angeles.

How much destruction, in terms of life and property, will the coming superquake in California cause? No one knows for certain, partly because the extent of damage will depend on the exact magnitude and focus of the tremor, details that cannot be foreseen, and partly because the United States has had no experience of such earthquakes for almost a century. There have been substantial earthquakes in the forty-eight contiguous United States over the past several decades, but none approaching the magnitude of the "city buster" that is expected to strike California in the near future.

The history of California is, to a large extent, a history of earthquakes. Here is a partial listing of major California tremors of the past two centuries:

Circa 1790. Native Americans told early European settlers about a powerful earthquake in Owens Valley about this time, but the exact date could not be determined.

October 11, 1800. Strong earthquakes shook San Juan Bautista and continued through the end of the month. No building escaped damage, and deep fissures appeared in the ground.

June 21, 1808. San Francisco's Presidio was shaken by a series of approximately twenty earthquakes that lasted until July 17. Unreinforced adobe structures were seriously damaged.

December 21,1812. Detailed information on this earthquake is hard to find, but it appears to have been centered offshore near Santa Barbara. This quake generated a tsunami, or seismic sea wave, that came ashore as a gigantic breaker. The wave is said to have picked up one ship, swept it inland along a canyon, then carried it back to sea. Mission Santa Barbara was totally destroyed.

1822 (date uncertain). A strong quake damaged Mission Santa Clara and Mission San Jose.

June 10, 1836. At 7:30 A.M., the San Francisco Bay area was shaken by one of the strongest quakes in its history. The ground was fissured along the East Bay from Mission San Jose to San Pablo. Aftershocks (smaller tremors following the principal earthquake) continued for several weeks.

June 1838. A very strong earthquake damaged the Presidio in San Francisco.

July 3, 1841. A major tremor was felt in Monterey and on ships offshore at about 2:00 P.M.

May 15, 1851. Shortly after 8:00 A.M., San Franciscans felt a moderately strong earthquake. Plaster fell from ceilings, and some buildings suffered serious damage.

November 22, 1852. A severe earthquake hit the San Francisco peninsula just before noon. The ground southwest of San Francisco was so deeply fissured that the waters of Lake Merced drained into the sea.

February 15, 1856. A powerful earthquake damaged buildings in San Francisco and agitated the waters of the bay. The quake was felt as far away as Stockton.

January 9, 1857. This tremor, commonly called the "Fort Tejon earthquake," was probably the strongest to hit California since Europeans arrived there. Accounts of the quake are fragmentary because the area was lightly settled at the time, but anecdotal evidence indicates this quake released perhaps twenty thousand times the energy of the 1945 nuclear explosion at Hiroshima.

The Fort Tejon earthquake was felt for almost the entire length and width of California, from San Diego in the south to points north of Sacramento, and from the coast near Los Angeles to the heart of the Sierra Nevada. In San Francisco, the earthquake was felt as a sudden, hard shock and was strong enough to toss sleepers from their beds. The quake was strong enough to frighten the townspeople of Yuma, Arizona, some three hundred miles east of Los Angeles.

Fort Tejon was an army installation built at Tejon Pass in the Tehachapi Mountains for defense against Mexicans and Native Americans. At the time of the earthquake, Fort Tejon was still under construction. The buildings were made of adobe, dried mud reinforced with straw or twigs. It was a poor choice of material, as the army was about to discover.

The officer in charge of Fort Tejon was Lt. Col. B. L. Beall, a middle-aged career man who was known in nearby Los Angeles as an upstanding citizen and a competent officer. He appears to have been the model of an army officer, a man for whom the welfare of those under his command took priority.

Beall must have thought all of nature was conspiring against him that January day. The weather at the lofty altitude of Tejon Pass was bitterly cold, and at 6:00 A.M. the ground began to shake energetically.

That in itself was not unusual. Earthquakes were familiar phenomena at Fort Tejon. Only five years earlier, in 1852, a severe earthquake had shaken the same land on which the Fort was built. In fact, the earth in the vicinity of the post was so notorious for destructive quakes that the army's inspector general had argued, before Fort Tejon was built, that Tejon Pass was too quake-prone to make a post there feasible.

But the quakes continued, at intervals of about five minutes, until an extremely powerful shock at 8:23 A.M. demolished many of the buildings on the post and severely damaged the remainder. Only a few of the quarters on the post remained habitable. No one was killed, because everyone at the fort had moved outdoors as soon as the quakes began.

It was the worst possible time to evacuate the post. The fierce chill outdoors caused even healthy men discomfort and posed a serious danger to several sick soldiers, who had to be moved into tents. In view of the cold weather, it was ironic that Beall also had to worry about the danger of fire; all the chimneys on the post had been damaged and were unsafe to use.

To make matters worse, Beall knew that for an indefinite period it would be risky to move any of his men back into the adobe structures on the base. At any moment another strong shock could bring the whole fort tumbling down on top of anyone who happened to be indoors.

Beall provided as best he could for the safety and warmth of his troops. That evening he sat down in one of the less severely damaged buildings and wrote his report of the disaster by candlelight. He told his superior, the army commanding general at Benecia, about the disaster and the hardship it was causing his men. He promised to report in person at Benecia as soon as he could board a ship leaving from Los Angeles. The following morning he wrote in a postscript that "during the night . . . the shocks have continued with much violence," and that buildings at the post "have been much damaged since 8:00 P.M. . . . yesterday." Then he sent off the report by special messenger and prepared to embark for Benecia.

That dreadful night was merely the beginning of the soldiers' suffering at Fort Tejon. They had to spend the remainder of the winter in their tents, under conditions similar to what Washington's troops endured at Valley Forge three-quarters of a century before. The shattered buildings remained uninhabitable, and there was no way to rebuild them during the winter; the only construction material available was adobe, and adobe could not be made from the frozen earth.

The army learned two important lessons from the Fort Tejon earthquake. One was to rebuild the fort at a lower altitude, outside Tejon Pass itself. The other lesson was to build the new fort out of more durable material than crumbly adobe. Though adobe was fire-resistant—an important consideration in the mid-1800s, when most indoor heating came from stoves and hearths—it was so friable that it offered virtually no resistance to the stresses produced by earthquakes. The dangers of adobe construction soon became clear but unfortunately had to be relearned time and again at communities all over California in the early days of European settlement there. It is difficult to say how many lives were lost in California from collapsing adobe structures, but the toll probably runs well into the thousands. One could argue that adobe architecture in quake-prone regions was responsible for as many deaths as gunfighting.

Though the people of Los Angeles did not have to contend with freezing weather on the day of the Fort Tejon quake (it was a warm, sunny day in Los Angeles), the one thousand or so residents of the community were terrified. The strongest shock, which came shortly after 8:30 A.M., killed one elderly woman who presumably was caught indoors when a building collapsed on her. Pedestrians on the street had trouble standing. Some horses panicked and escaped from their corrals; others lay down on the ground to wait for the quake to pass. Livestock outside the city suffered from the quake as well— ranchers reported herds of cattle stampeding even before the shocks began.

The most detailed report of the earthquake was published in 1876 in a newspaper in nearby Visalia. The paper called it the "heaviest earthquake shock . . . ever experienced" in the San Joaquin Valley and described the event vividly: "Houses and trees vibrated violently. The solid earth seemed to have lost its stability, and a wavelike motion was experienced as on shipboard. . . . Nature seemed filled with terror." One man in the San Fernando Valley said afterward that the ground "was in fearful agitation, with undulations so quick and rapid as to make it almost impossible to stand. The sensation was very much like that felt on the deck of a small vessel in a heavy chopped sea."

Residents of Los Angeles and neighboring communities saw their houses sway and crumble as the shock waves passed through the ground below. But many homes were spared because the motion of the earth was slow; consequently, buildings had a chance to catch their breath, so to speak, between jolts. Damage "would have been appalling," one eyewitness wrote, if the shock had been more sudden.

According to newspaper accounts, cracks several feet wide opened in the ground just south of Los Angeles, and a miner near Fort Tejon looked on in astonishment as the earth beside him gaped open and swallowed his camping equipment. Streams had their courses changed at Paredes. The Mokelumne River was literally thrown from its bed, exposing the bottom, while the Kern River reversed its flow and slopped over its banks in four-foot waves. Groundwater spurted six feet into the air from fissures along the Santa Clara River. The Los Angeles River spilled out onto the adjacent floodplain, and the quake divided the San Gabriel River into two forks.

There was even a report of mild volcanic activity associated with the Fort Tejon earthquake. Steam under pressure was said to have burst from a fissure in the ground near San Fernando, and the earth around the crack was allegedly too hot to touch. It is hard to tell whether this report is accurate or imaginary because the public in the 1850s tended to associate earthquakes almost inseparably with volcanoes. So the author of this report of steaming earth may simply have assumed there was volcanic activity near Los Angeles during the earthquake and written his supposition down as fact.

When all reports of the earthquake were collected and analyzed, the scope of the damage, to human-built structures and to the natural landscape, was astonishing. The Fort Tejon earthquake had ruptured the ground for at least 275 miles along the California coast. The ruptures followed the course of the now famous San Andreas Fault, which has given California some of its most devastating earthquakes. We will see more of the San Andreas Fault later, since it is practically synonymous with the earthquake threat now hanging over Los Angeles.

November 26, 1858. Virtually every brick or masonry structure in San Jose was damaged by an earthquake that occurred a few minutes after midnight. Buildings constructed on landfill in San Francisco also suffered damage.

July 3, 1861. Workers in fields were knocked off their feet by an earthquake near Livermore.

March 5, 1864. An earthquake in San Francisco shattered store windows.

March 8, 1865. Clocks were stopped and chimneys knocked down by an earthquake near Santa Rosa.

October 8, 1865. A few minutes after noon, one of the most powerful earthquakes in California history destroyed numerous buildings in San Francisco, notably the Old Merchants' Exchange Building at the corner of Battery and Washington streets. A fissure two blocks long appeared in the ground along Howard Street. The earthquake also caused extensive landslides in the Santa Cruz Mountains.

March 26, 1866. An early afternoon earthquake was felt clearly in the San Francisco area, but damage appears to have been minimal.

October 21, 1868. Some thirty persons in the San Francisco area were killed by a major earthquake centered near San Leandro on this bright Sunday morning. Every building in Hayward was damaged, and many were totally destroyed. The quake was felt more than 150 miles away. Mount Tamalpais, north of San Francisco, was displaced several feet by the earthquake, and buildings constructed on geologically unstable landfill in San Francisco were upset and shattered as the quake rippled through the ground beneath them. Mark Twain was working as a newspaperman in San Francisco at that time, and his description of the earthquake is one of the most vivid ever put to paper:

> It was just after noon [when] I was coming down Third Street. The only objects in motion anywhere in that thickly built and populous quarter were a man in a buggy behind me and a streetcar wending slowly up a cross street. Otherwise all was solitude and a Sabbath stillness. As I turned a corner around a frame house, there was a great rattle and jar, and it occurred to me that here was an item—no doubt a fight in that house.
>
> Before I could turn and seek the door, there came a really terrific shock; the ground seemed to roll underneath me in waves, interrupted by a violent joggling up and down. There was a heavy grinding noise as of brick houses rubbing together. I fell up against the frame house and hurt my elbow. I knew what it was by this time and from mere reportorial instinct, nothing else, took out my watch and noted the time of day. At that moment a third and still more severe shock came; as I reeled about on the pavement, trying to keep my footing, I saw sights both tragic and comic.

Twain noticed the streetcar had stopped. The horses were rearing and bucking while passengers rushed out both ends of the car. One man, Twain saw, had "crashed halfway through a glass window on one side of the car, got wedged fast, and was . . . squealing like an impaled madman."

Every doorway of every house, Twain reported, was "vomiting a stream of human beings," so that in an instant "there was a massed multitude of people stretching in endless procession" down every street he could see. "Never," Twain remarked, "was solemn solitude turned into teeming life more quickly." Late sleepers "thronged into the public streets in all manner of queer apparel, and some without any at all. One woman who had been washing a naked child ran down the street holding it by the ankles as if it had been a dressed turkey."

The quake upset the lives of everyone from pool sharks to shavers. Twain told how San Franciscans "who were supposed to keep the Sabbath strictly rushed out of saloons in their shirt-sleeves, with billiard cues in their hands. Dozens of men [ran outside] with their necks swathed in napkins, lathered to the eyes, or with one cheek shaved clean and the other still bearing a heavy stubble."

Twain also observed animals' reactions to the earthquake. "Horses broke from stables," he wrote, "and a frightened dog rushed up a short attic ladder and onto a roof and when his scare was over had not the nerve to go down again the same way he had come up."

Damage to buildings was severe, as Twain noted: "The plastering that fell from ceilings in San Francisco that day would have covered acres of ground." He also described how a fissure "a hundred feet long gaped open six inches wide in the middle of the street, and then shut together again with such force as to ridge up the meeting earth like a slender grave." Twain continued:

> The first shock brought down two or three huge organ pipes in one of the chuches. The minister, with uplifted hands, was just closing the services. He glanced up, hesitated, and said, "However, we will omit the benediction." In the next instant, there was a vacancy in the atmosphere where he had stood.
>
> After the first shock, an Oakland minister said, "Keep your seats. There is no better place to die than this," but then added after a second, "But outside is good enough." He then skipped out the back door.

Pictures hung by wires on the wall, Twain said, "were . . . by a curious freak of the earthquake's humor, whirled around completely with [their] faces to the wall." He added that "thousands of people were made so seasick by the rolling and pitching of floors and streets that they were weak and bedridden for hours, and some for even days afterward. Hardly an individual escaped [motion sickness] entirely."

March 26, 1872. The Owens Valley earthquake on this date was one of California's most destructive and spectacular quakes. It broke the surface for about one hundred miles, between Olancha and Big Pine, and in some locations the earth was uplifed more than twenty feet. The initial shock was the strongest; it created a mighty wave in Owens Lake and dried up the Owens River for a few hours. At one bridge, passersby saw fish tossed out of the water and onto the bank by the shock. Calmly, they picked up the fish and proceeded to cook them for breakfast.

The Owens Valley quake illustrated dramatically the weakness of adobe for construction. The community of Lone Pine was built entirely of adobe structures, every last one of which was destroyed, killing twenty-three persons. Nearby Fort Independence fared better; though it, too, was an adobe-home settlement, no one was killed there, and only one person was injured.

In Yosemite Valley, the earthquake awakened John Muir, the famous naturalist who coined the saying, "Bring me men to match my mountains!" Muir was asleep in his little cabin near Sentinel Rock when the quake struck. He wrote later: "At half-past two o'clock . . . I was awakened by a tremendous earthquake . . . the strange thrilling motion could not be mistaken, and I ran out of my cabin, both glad and frightened, shouting, 'A noble earthquake! A noble earthquake!' feeling sure I was going to learn something."

He did learn something: earthquakes were dangerous as well as noble. All around him, by the bright moonlight, Muir saw boulders shaken loose by the quake tumble down to the valley floor. Muir took shelter behind a tree. After the quake subsided, he went down to the nearby Merced River to see if the river had altered its flow. The riverbed looked unchanged, and Muir said he "was glad to find that DOWN the valley was still DOWN."

An hour later another earthquake shook the valley. The shocks continued for eight weeks. Muir had no scientific instruments for studying the quakes, so he improvised a primitive quake detector: a bucket of water sitting on a table. When the water in the pail began to oscillate and splash, Muir knew a quake was coming.

March 6, 1882, and March 30, 1883. Two strong quakes at Hollister broke windows and dislodged plaster.

March 30, 1885. An earthquake at Mulberry, southeast of Hollister, toppled chimneys and caused extensive fissuring of the ground along the Pajaro and San Benito rivers.

May 19, 1889. Much of central California was shaken by a quake centered near Antioch, where glass was broken and chimneys were damaged.

April 14, 1890. The great "nonquake" that was predicted for this date illustrates how edgy Californians had become concerning earthquakes as the nineteenth century was ending. Early in 1890, a self-styled prophet named Cricksor declared that San Francisco and Oakland would both be destroyed by earthquakes on April 14. For good measure, he added that quakes also would level New York and Chicago at the same time. Cricksor's prophecy casued great alarm in San Francisco; property values plummeted, and some fearful souls moved out of town to escape what they saw as impending doom. But the earthquake failed to occur as predicted. A powerful quake did strike Hollister on April 24 and displaced the railroad bridge over the Pajaro River, but that earthquake made Cricksor's prediction ten days too early and more than a hundred miles off, and his reputation as a seer was irretrievably damaged. Similar incidents of "earthquake prophecy" have occurred in recent years in California. Psychics had a field day in the late 1960s, during a national obsession with the occult, trying to foretell when the next major quake would strike California. Some soothsayers said disaster would strike San Francisco; others pointed to Los Angeles as the most likely spot. Yet as the last seconds of the sixties ticked away, both cities were still standing. To be fair to the psychics, however, let it be said that their record of successful quake predictions is about as good as that of legitimate scientists, for reasons we will explore in a later chapter.

October 11, 1891. Residents of the Napa Valley had just retired for the night when a major earthquake shook them out of their beds.

April 19, 1892. The town of Vacaville was practically wiped off the map by an earthquake, which was felt as far away as western Nevada. An aftershock on April 21 was felt in Reno, Nevada.

March 30, 1898. An earthquake at 11:43 P.M. wrecked the Mare Island Navy Yard. There would have been numerous fatalities if the quake had occurred a few hours earlier.

July 22, 1899. A quake near Cajon Pass in the San Bernardino Mountains covered a highway with fallen rock for almost half a mile. A man named Baker learned from this earthquake that quakes can create unusual hazards. A newspaper noted that Baker was being shaved in a barbershop in San Bernardino when the earthquake began. "He was badly frightened," the paper reported, "and rising suddenly from his chair, his face came in contact with the razor, the result being a long deep gash." As a surgeon stitched shut the wound, an aftershock made Baker jump again. This time he was jabbed painfully by the surgeon's needle.

December 25, 1899. This was a sad Christmas Day for San Jacinto, where six persons were killed by collapsing buildings during an earthquake.

July 27, 1902. Los Alamos (not to be confused with the site of the modern nuclear weapons research laboratory in New Mexico) was evacuated by train when a series of strong quakes began to shake the community. On their return, the townspeople found every building damaged, every chimney thrown down, and the streets broken and fissured. Underground oil pipes at Lompoc were destroyed, and aboveground oil pipes were bent and broken.

April 18, 1906. The 1906 San Francisco earthquake has been the subject of dozens of books, several motion pictures, and hundreds of articles but never loses its fascination for scientists or the ordinary citizen. It marked the end of an era for San Francisco: the pre-earthquake time in which San Francisco enjoyed a unique combination of industry and indolence, innocence and decadence, provincialism and cosmopolitanism. No one has described the atmosphere of those days in San Francisco better than New York author Will Irwin:

> It was a city of romance and . . . adventure. It opened
> out on the mysterious Pacific, the untamed ocean, and
> most of China, Japan, and the South Sea Islands, lower

California, the west coast of Central America, [and] Australia that came to this country passed in through the Golden Gate. There was a sprinkling, too, of Alaska and Siberia. . . . San Francisco was the back eddy of European civilization—one end of the world.

Prior to the 1906 earthquake, San Francisco had plenty of warning that such an event was possible. In the previous fifty years, more than four hundred earthquakes were recorded in the San Francisco Bay region. Two of them, in 1865 and 1868, were strong enough to cause serious damage to buildings. San Franciscans were also cautioned that their city stood to burn down in the event of a major earthquake; just several months before the 1906 disaster, the National Board of Fire Underwriters issued a pessimistic report on fire safety in San Francisco, describing the city as "a catastrophe waiting to happen" and pointing out that its water supply was inadequate to fight a calamitous blaze. Here is an excerpt from the report:

> In view of the exceptionally large areas, great heights, numerous unprotected openings, general absence of fire breaks or stops, [and] highly combustible nature of the buildings, the potential [fire] hazard is very severe.
>
> The above features combined with the almost total lack of sprinklers and absence of modern protective devices generally, numerous and mutually aggravating conflagration breeders, high winds, and comparatively narrow streets, make the probability . . . [of fire] alarmingly severe.
>
> In fact, San Francisco has violated all underwriting traditions by not burning up. That it has not done so is largely due to the vigilance of the fire department, which cannot be relied upon indefinitely to stave off the inevitable [conflagration].

Yet San Franciscans paid little heed to these warnings. Then as now, San Francisco was a city that lived for the moment, and its residents—"perfectly mad people," Rudyard Kipling called them after a visit to California—were much too busy making money and pursuing pleasure to consider the chance of disaster ahead. "The city never went to bed," Irwin wrote. "There was no closing law, so that the saloons kept open nights and Sundays at their own sweet will."

Irwin told the story of the trouble that broke out one evening in the Eye Wink Dance Hall. A sailor named Kanaka Pete started a fight over a woman called Iodoform Kate. Pete chased his rival for Kate's affections to the Little Silver Dollar saloon and shot him dead. Several shots went wild and left holes in the front of the Eye Wink. The bullet marks "were proudly kept as souvenirs," said Irwin.

Not everyone in San Francisco, however, approved of its hedonistic ways. Early in 1906, Mary McDermitt, an evangelist with a religious cult called the Flying Rollers of the House of David, publicly denounced San Francisco for its impiety and called on God to send an earthquake on the city as a judgment. That prayer must have been widespread among the pious, for on the night of April 17, 1906, a Mormon elder named J. R. Shepard also grew outraged at what he saw as the sinful lifestyles of San Franciscans, and at a church social he prayed that his deity would cause "something awful to happen to San Francisco and make it receptive to God."

Several hours later, it appeared his prayer was answered.

All that night horses had been uneasy in their stalls, as if distressed by something humans could not hear or feel. They were upset by the early rumblings of a major earthquake: low-frequency vibrations imperceptible to humans, but disturbing to the more acute senses of livestock.

At 5:13 A.M., just before dawn, the earthquake struck. It announced its coming in San Francisco with a deep rumble. Then the shock wave from the quake became visible. One policeman described seeing the wave roll up Washington Street. "The whole street was undulating," he said. "It was as if the waves of the ocean were coming toward me, billowing as they came."

Another eyewitness described the quake thus: "a low, rumbling noise . . . as of the earth in agony . . . dying away to nothing, followed by a silence so keen that all nature seemed to stop to listen." The noise of the quake, he added, was accompanied by a "great smash and clash of groaning buildings, the creaking of battered walls, the snapping of steel, the cracking of glass, and the shrieks of [the] dying . . ." The screams of the wounded, he recalled, were "mingled with those of frightened horses."

Ships offshore were also troubled by the quake. A schooner 150 miles off the Golden Gate bounded upward in the water and then settled again, to the bafflement of her master and crew. This phenomenon was probably caused by a tsunami.

The initial tremor lasted forty seconds, then died away. The clanging of church bells rocked by the earthquake awakened anyone not already roused by the vibrations. Ten seconds later the earthquake resumed with even greater intensity and shook the city for about half a minute.

When the earth ceased rocking, much of San Francisco lay in ruins. Market Street, the city's main thoroughfare, was ripped apart, and its trolley tracks lay twisted like crawling snakes. Groundwater seeped up from fissures in the pavement. The stone facade of City Hall had collapsed, leaving the naked steel framework of the dome uncovered and huge ornamental columns scattered like so many toothpicks on the adjoining plaza.

All over the city shattered glass and broken stone cornices rained down on the streets, while homes built on landfill—that is, unconsolidated sediment—listed and crumbled as shock waves rippled through the soil beneath them. In the Mission district, the four-story Valencia Hotel collapsed like a soggy cake, killing as many as eighty guests (the exact number was never determined). Most of the victims at the hotel were not crushed but drowned in a first-floor flood caused by a ruptured water main.

A few miles away in the western addition, San Francisco's newly built residential district, St. Dominic's Church lost its elegant twin spires. Their exteriors shattered and fell away, exposing their steel supports. Only the top of one spire remained intact, poised atop its girders like a thimble balanced on a needle.

Near the Hall of Records downtown, homes stood canted at crazy angles. One entire row of two-story houses tilted away from the street at a forty-degree angle, like toppled stage scenery. Chinatown, where most buildings were made of cheap masonry, was virtually wiped out by the quake. Elsewhere the earthquake showed a startling selectivity in which homes it destroyed. On Howard Street, it was nothing unusual to find one house practically demolished and an adjacent house relatively unscathed, with little more damage than some fallen plaster and shattered glass.

When the earthquake hurled brick against wood, the results were often catastrophic. All over the city chimneys collapsed and fell through rooftops like aerial bombs, crushing anything and anyone below them. One observer at a hotel on Post Street watched the quake destroy several small wooden houses in this fashion. They collapsed "like emptied eggs," he said, when the bricks smashed through the roof.

The earthquake was one of the most vivid memories in the colorful life of tenor Enrico Caruso, who was in San Francisco to sing Don José in *Carmen* at the Opera House. Awakened by the quake in his room at the Palace Hotel ("I feel my bed rocking as though I am in a ship," he recalled later), Caruso looked from his window and saw buildings swaying and large chunks of masonry falling.

At first he was hysterical. His friend, conductor Alfred Hertz, checked Caruso's room and discovered the singer sitting on the bed weeping for fear that the catastrophe had somehow damaged his voice. The level-headed Hertz knew how to handle Caruso. Throwing open the window of Caruso's room, Hertz told him to stand before it and sing.

Caruso did so and found his voice intact. He launched into a selection from Giordano's *Fedora*, the opera that had catapulted him to international fame several years before. The tenor's impromptu performance reassured frightened townspeople in the street below. They looked up and applauded, delighted to see that their famous guest seemed unafraid.

Shortly afterward Caruso—his throat wrapped in towels to protect his vocal cords from the chill morning air—left the hotel to find safer quarters. From time to time he stopped to serenade passersby. Making his way toward the harbor and the relative security of a boat there, he met actor John Barrymore, who had been attending a private party at the time of the earthquake and was wandering around the streets in formal dress. Caruso burst out laughing when he saw Barrymore's attire. "Mr. Barrymore," Caruso said, "you are the only man in the world who would dress for an earthquake!" (Barrymore's biographer, Gene Fowler, writes that Barrymore persuaded a reporter to include with a news dispatch to New York a personal message to his sister, Ethel. Barrymore said, untruthfully, that he had been thrown from his bed by the earthquake, then forced by an army sergeant to wield a shovel among the ruins for twenty-four hours. Ethel read this unlikely report to her famous uncle, John Drew Barrymore, and asked him if he believed it. "Every word," he replied. "It took an act of God to get him out of bed and the United States Army to put him to work.")

Caruso at last reached the waterfront. He asked to board a boat there, but initially the crew didn't believe their visitor was the great Caruso. He convinced them by singing an aria. The crewmen welcomed Caruso on board, and he stood on the fantail as the boat chugged out into the harbor, away from the dangers on land. That night Caruso had to sleep on hard ground. "My legs ache yet from so rough a bed," he said later in his unorthodox English.

There are other accounts of Caruso's behavior that day, not all of them flattering. According to one story, the beefy tenor used a shotgun to commandeer a wagon for his trip, during which he is said to have remarked, *"Vesuvius, sì; San Francisco, no!"* (The volcanic mountain Vesuvius, in Caruso's native Italy, had erupted five days before the San Francisco earthquake.)

Caruso was acquitted of this canard in 1983 by the California Court of Historical Review and Appeals, a nonofficial tribunal set up in 1975 by a local judge and a publicist to increase public interest in San Francisco history. The "court" ruled that Caruso had not behaved disgracefully that morning in 1906, nor had he slandered San Francisco. On the contrary, the ruling stated, Caruso left San Francisco with his fondness for the city intact and was planning to return in 1921, when he died of a lung disorder in Italy.

A few miles south of San Francisco, the famous Harvard University psychologist and author William James was staying at Stanford University while delivering a course of lectures there. Before James left Massachusetts for California, one of his colleagues at Harvard said to him jokingly, "Maybe they'll give you a touch of earthquake while you are there." James remembered that jest on the morning of April 18. He described the earthquake thus:

When lying awake at about half-past five [in] the morning . . . in my little flat on the campus of Stanford, I felt the bed begin to waggle; my first consciousness was one of gleeful recognition of the nature of the movement. "By Jove," I said to myself, "here's [the] earthquake after all!" And then as it went *crescendo*, "And a jolly good one it is, too," I said.

Sitting up involuntarily, and taking a kneeling position, I was thrown down on my face as it went *fortior*. . . . Then everything that was on anything else slid off to the floor, over went the bureau and chiffonier with a crash, and the *fortissimo* was reached.

Another renowned eyewitness to the quake that morning was novelist Jack London, best-selling author of *White Fang* and *The Call of the Wild*. A few weeks earlier, London, a rabid socialist for much of his life, said frankly what he thought of wealthy San Franciscans and their lifestyle of conspicuous consumption: "Someday, when we get a few more hands and crowbars to work, we'll topple it over, along with all its rotten life and unburied dead, its monstrous selfishness and sodden materialism."

The earthquake did that task for him. At his farm in Sonoma County, London woke up just in time to hear the crash of his brick silo—the first such silo in northern California—as it fell in ruins.

London and his wife, Charmian, got on their horses and rode toward the destroyed city. When they arrived, even the prolific London found himself at a loss for words. "I'll never write about this for anybody," he said. "What use trying? One could only string big words together and curse the futility of them." But a lucrative offer from *Collier's* magazine changed his mind, and London started scribbling down his impressions of the earthquake. Charmian typed them, and London dropped the manuscript in the mail.

Then as now, mail service was not always reliable, and the manuscript seems to have taken its sweet time getting to *Collier's*. For the next week, London was bombarded by frantic wires from the East. "Why doesn't your story arrive?" the magazine demanded. "Holding presses at enormous expense. What is the matter?"

At last the article arrived. It appeared in the May 5 issue and began:

> San Francisco is gone! Nothing remains of it but memories and a fringe of dwelling houses on its outskirts. . . . All the cunning adjustments of a twentieth-century city [were] smashed by the earthquake.

But London was seeing only the aftermath of the earthquake. He had not been there for the actual event. The following quotes from eyewitnesses to the quake provide some idea of what those terrifying few seconds were like:

> I saw buildings fly up in the air and become fragments, like shells hurtled from mammoth guns. I saw wrought iron and steel twisted and bent in the strangest conceivable shapes.

> My room was in the Grand Hotel. When I awakened, the house was shaking as a terrier would shake a rat. . . . Then I saw the first dead come by. They were piled up in an automobile like carcasses in a butcher's wagon, all over bloody, with crushed skulls and broken limbs and bloody faces.

> The floor rocked like a boat on a choppy sea, but the violence of the motion increased and seemed ever and again to take a fresh start. It seemed as if it would never end, and yet it lasted but two minutes.

Awakened by the earthquake, Helen Dare jumped out of bed and tried to keep her balance. She had the illusion that the far wall of her bedroom was moving away from her. Her young son ran into the room, and they stood holding each other for several minutes in the doorway. Then, after the earthquake was over, they dressed and got out of the building.

Dare and her son saw masses of terrified San Franciscans heading for the nearby hills. They were afraid a tsunami might sweep in from the sea, and they wanted to be safe on high ground if and when the wave arrived. Near the waterfront, a large gas tank had exploded and was burning; some people,

Dare was told, thought the earthquake had actually been the shock wave released when the tank blew up.

The Dares continued walking, down Pacific Avenue and then Van Ness Avenue. At the homes of several wealthy townsfolk, they saw something that was astonishing and reassuring at the same time. Though their homes had been shattered by the earthquake, the upper crust had simply moved a few chairs outdoors and were having their customary morning tea seated on the sidewalk. Nothing, it seemed, could crack the aplomb of San Francisco's ruling class.

Farther along, Dare witnessed a tableau of agony at the front door of a bank. A man—evidently the manager—stood on the front steps, fidgeting and crying out, "Why doesn't he come? Will he never come with the combination?"

At the Presidio in San Francisco, Brigadier General Frederick Funston exceeded his legitimate authority immediately after the quake by declaring martial law, a measure that only the president of the United States was entitled to invoke. Later Funston would be criticized severely for his handling of the crisis. To keep the city from being sacked, his troops were given orders to shoot looters on sight. As Mayor E. E. Schmitz said in an official proclamation, "The federal troops, the members of our regular police force, and all special police officers have been authorized to kill any and all persons found engaged in looting or in the commission of any other crime."

But overzealous soldiers were not always careful to distinguish between looters and displaced homeowners, and some San Franciscans were shot by mistake while trying to salvage their belongings from the rubble of their own homes. Suspected looters were treated in a fashion that would be condemned as brutality today. The *Chronicle* reported on April 21 that two thieves were tied together and thrown into a cemetery to await a more convenient opportunity to convey them to jail. "When the officer in command of the squad arrived on the scene, he expressed indignation that the two looters had not been shot at once," the paper noted.

Yet disorder was rare in the city. London noted that while the city fell in ruins, "the most perfect courtesy obtained. Never in all San Francisco's history were her people so kind and courteous as on this night of terror." Other eyewitnesses confirmed London's observation. In the Latin Quarter, for example, the crowds remained eminently calm, even while crowding into the middle of the street to avoid harm from falling brickwork.

After the last vibrations of the quake died away, wild rumors began to flit like bats through San Francisco. The whole country (they said) was stricken. Los Angeles was aflame. So were New York and Chicago. The Pacific Northwest had slid into the ocean. Giant waves had inundated the whole East Coast. Europe was reeling from a great volcanic eruption. (This rumor probably was inspired by the eruption of Vesuvius earlier in April.) As it happened, the San Francisco quake was hardly felt at all east of the Rockies; but to survivors on the city's streets, it must have seemed as if earthquake and fire were about to destroy the world.

Fire did consume much of San Francisco in the days just after the quake, as the underwriters' report had predicted. Shortly after the tremors ceased, a cooking fire in the slum area south of Market Street burned out of control, and before long a sizable portion of San Francisco was in flames. No water was available for fire fighting, because the mains that serviced the city had been broken by the earthquake. To halt the fire's advance, firemen and soldiers tried to create firebreaks by blowing up buildings.

General Funston's men have received much of the blame for the rapid spread of the fire. It is widely believed that their blasting set off fires because the army men had little experience in handling explosives. That may be partly true, but a more important factor was the explosive they used. The soldiers had only a few hundred sticks of ordinary dynamite, supplied by the city's engineering department, and those were soon used up. The only alternative was an explosive called "giant powder." It was dynamite, too, but granulated like sugar or cereal. Giant powder was highly incendiary, much more so than ordinary dynamite, and tended to set fire to whatever it blew up.

That was exactly what it did to buildings in San Francisco. When the powder went off, it ignited anything inflammable in the structures it destroyed. Thus the blasting created more fires than it prevented, if it prevented any at all. At last the desperate soldiers turned to their artillerymen for help, and homes along Van Ness Avenue were shelled to the ground. Even this drastic measure was ineffective. The fire continued to advance.

Fire Chief Dennis Sullivan was not present to lead his men,

for he died tragically in the quake. He lived with his wife in an apartment on the top floor of the Bush Street firehouse next to the California Hotel. As the initial shock rippled through the city, heavy ornamental stonework from the hotel shook loose and crashed through the firehouse roof. One chunk of stone landed on Mrs. Sullivan's bed and sent it crashing—with her aboard—three stories down to the ground. She suffered only slight injuries, but Chief Sullivan was caught under a cascade of falling masonry as he rushed into his wife's bedroom to aid her. Sullivan was pulled alive from the rubble, but he fell into a coma and expired a few hours later.

As Sullivan lay dying, the fire swept through San Francisco. Initially three different fires were involved. One started south of Market Street, one along Market Street itself, and a third in Hayes Valley, several miles away. The fires were the greatest social levelers San Francisco had ever seen; they showed no respect for color, creed, or class. The flames consumed hovels and hotels, mansions and marble palaces alike. Not even the homes of millionaires on Nob Hill were saved. The Mark Hopkins mansion went up in flames, as did the great stone palace built by railroad magnate Collis P. Huntington, who is said to have served as the model for a fictional robber baron in Frank Norris's famous novel *McTeague*. Hopkins and Huntington were spared the agony of seeing their homes destroyed: both men had died several years before.

London described a conversation he had with a prosperous businessman as the fire advanced on the merchant's home:

> He was cool and cheerful and hospitable. "Yesterday morning," he said, "I was worth six hundred thousand dollars. This morning, this house is all I have left. It will go in fifteen minutes." He pointed to a large cabinet. "That is my wife's collection of china. This rug upon which we stand is a present. It cost fifteen hundred dollars. Try that piano. Listen to its tone. There are few like it. There are no horses. The flames will be here in fifteen minutes."

Outside, as London and the merchant spoke, the Mark Hopkins mansion was catching fire. Troops were herding refugees out of the area. Later, in Union Square, London saw a man offering a thousand dollars for a team of horses. The man was in charge of a wagon full of trunks from a hotel. The cargo had been hauled to Union Square because it seemed a safe place, and the horses had been taken away. Now fire was advancing on Union Square from three sides, and no horses were available.

Near the truck stood an elderly man on crutches. London urged him to flee from the approaching blaze and received a heartbreaking reply. "Today is my birthday," said the old man. "Last night I was worth thirty thousand dollars. . . . [Now] all I own are these crutches." London persuaded him to seek safety. A few minutes later London looked back and saw the trunks blazing in the street.

On Mission Street, London saw a dozen cooked steers—literally cooked—lying where they had been killed by falling debris during the earthquake. "The fire," London wrote, "had passed through afterward and roasted them." Farther along Mission Street, London saw where the driver of a milk wagon had narrowly escaped death. A steel telegraph pole had fallen across the driver's seat and smashed it. Milk cans lay scattered in the street.

San Franciscans did their best to save their possessions. Some preserved their belongings successfully by putting them in trunks and burying the trunks in their backyards, to be recovered after the fire. Others tried to lug the trunks with them as they fled the fire. "Over these trunks many a strong man broke his heart," London wrote. He described soldiers retreating before the flames and prodding trunk haulers to move on. London recalled later how exhausted men at bayonet point would "arise and struggle up the steep pavements, pausing from weakness every five or ten feet." To lighten the load, the refugees would discard one precious possession after another, until their belongings were reduced to almost nothing at all. Some families were left with only enough possessions to fill a baby buggy or a toy wagon.

Bankers in San Francisco had to evacuate their offices as fire consumed the downtown business district. A. P. Giannini, president of the Bank of Italy—later to become the mighty Bank of America—piled his institution's assets into a horse-drawn cart and hauled them away just ahead of the advancing flames. Crocker Bank employees tossed $1 million in bonds into a wheelbarrow and carried them to a boat, which was sailed into the middle of the bay and anchored there until it was safe to return to shore. From that vantage point, the bankers might have been able to see Father Charles Ramm climbing the spire of St. Mary's Cathedral to beat out fires on the roof.

Residents of San Francisco's Italian district used a different and highly effective tactic to keep flames from spreading to their rooftops. As the fire approached, someone in the neighborhood cried out, "There's a last chance, boys!" The Italians understood immediately. They dashed to their cellars, where a small ocean of wine was stored, and broke in the barrel heads. Bucket brigades were formed to carry the wine from cellar to roof, and sheets and sacks dipped in the wine were used to extinguish fires as fast as they could start. "The wine won," one newspaper reported, and the paper praised "the lads . . . [who] went thirsty to save the wine to pour on the fire." As the Italians fought with wet sacks to save their homes, other San Franciscans tried different methods to stop the fire. One bearded man stood in the street holding a picture of St. Francis, the city's namesake, calling out to the saint and imploring him to save San Francisco from burning.

The city's parks and public squares began to fill up with refugees from the fire. In Union Square, exhausted men and women fleeing the fire south of Market Street stretched out on the grass and fell asleep at the foot of the monument to Admiral Dewey. Many of the displaced persons were transients who had been forced to flee their hotels. Not all of them seemed dismayed. One group of refugees in Union Square seemed to be having grand fun watching their city burn. They moved a piano into the square and stood around it, singing merrily. What they sang is uncertain, but "Hot Time in the Old Town Tonight" is a good possibility.

That night indeed was warm in San Francisco. And that was remarkable, because April nights there are usually chilly and foggy. But the heat of the fire was so intense that it changed the city's climate temporarily and drove away the cold and mist.

As the fire made its way through downtown San Francisco, the city's newspapers—the *Call, Chronicle,* and *Examiner*—rose to the occasion. Reporters dutifully filed their stories on the disaster, and the journals prepared to go to press. But the fire intervened. At the towering *Call* building on Market Street (the first skyscraper in the western United States), the steam-powered presses were unable to run because no water was available to fill the boilers.

Even with water for steam, however, the pressmen could never have put out an edition. As the staff pondered what to do next, gas in a sewer running in front of the building exploded. A manhole cover sailed through the air and into the *Call* building, demolishing the typesetting equipment.

Moreover, the building stood directly in the path of the advancing fire. The *Call* editors could see their building was doomed. So was the *Examiner* building nearby. The *Call* and *Examiner* bosses held a hasty conference with their colleagues at the *Chronicle* and decided to ask for aid from the Oakland *Tribune* across the bay.

A few minutes later the *Call* building was ablaze. The round windows that ringed its ornate cupola glowed orange, like huge jack-o'-lanterns, as the fire ravaged the building's insides. Then the windows blew out with a noise like gunshots as the flames heated air within the skyscraper to explosive pressure. Green flame burst from the sixth floor. Soon the whole building was aflame.

But it took more than earthquake and fire to stop San Francisco's newsmen. One day after the earthquake, April 19, the *Call, Chronicle,* and *Examiner* pooled their resources to put out a joint morning edition. Headlines from it reveal something of San Francisco's pitiable state:

EARTHQUAKE AND FIRE: SAN FRANCISCO IN RUINS

NO HOPE LEFT FOR SAFETY OF ANY BUILDINGS

BLOW BUILDINGS UP TO CHECK FLAMES

WHOLE CITY IS ABLAZE

NEWSPAPER ROW IS GUTTED

PANIC-STRICKEN PEOPLE FLEE

DEAD IN STREET

DAMAGE A BILLION

The lead front-page story recounted San Francisco's plight in purple prose:

> Death and destruction have been the fate of San Francisco. Shaken . . . and scourged by flames that

raged diametrically in all directions, the city is a mass of smoldering ruins. . . . Downtown everything is ruin. Not a business house stands. Theaters are crumbled into heaps. Factories and commission houses lie smoldering on their former sites. All of the newspaper sites have been rendered useless. . . .

As the flames consumed San Francisco, London found himself at one point sitting on a boat offshore, watching a peculiar phenomenon that he dubbed the "suck":

It was dead calm. Not a flicker of wind stirred. Yet from every side wind was pouring in upon the city. East, west, north, and south, strong winds were blowing in upon the doomed city. The heated air rising made an enormous suck. Thus did the fire of itself build its own colossal chimney through the atmosphere. Day and night this dead calm continued, and yet, near to the flames, the wind was often half a gale, so mighty was the suck.

Modern scientists refer to this "suck" as a "convection current." It is created when a heat source on the ground—in this case, the fire—warms air above it and causes the air to rise, creating an upward draft. This process is called convection, and it is responsible for, among other things, the mushroom-shaped clouds of nuclear explosions. And had London been able to foresee the coming age of atomic warfare, he probably would have compared the burning city to the aftermath of an A-bomb blast.

Thousands of other San Franciscans followed London's example and made their way toward the perceived safety of the waterfront. Overcrowded ferries were hauling load after load of refugees across the bay to Oakland. Looking back at the burning city, they watched as the three individual fires in San Francisco finally merged into one huge, dark gray pillar of smoke, through which the sun shone as a dim red disc.

Smoke hung thick in the air above Market Street as a long line of men and women trudged silently toward the ferry slips at the Embarcadero, which the fire thus far had spared. But on the afternoon of April 19, the fire advanced on the waterfront, and the refugees had to turn back to the western part of town. From across the bay observers watched as huge clouds of dark smoke began to rise from Meig's Wharf, which was located about where Fisherman's Wharf is today. The spire of the Ferry Building was visible whenever the smoke parted briefly.

Among the areas devastated by the fire was the so-called Barbary Coast, the iniquitous stretch of waterfront that was largely responsible for giving San Francisco society a notorious name back east. (The area is now known as Jackson Square.) "This was low life," one eastern journalist described the Barbary Coast, "the lowest of the low." The expression "shanghai," meaning to abduct a person for service on ships bound for China, is said to have originated here. Whether or not it actually did, the denizens of the Barbary Coast surely perfected the practice. One saloon built on a pier had a trapdoor cut in front of the bar especially to shanghai customers. As an unfortunate patron knocked back his drink, the trapdoor opened under his feet, and he dropped into a waiting boat below, where he was knocked unconscious and hauled off to servitude at sea.

The businessmen of the Barbary Coast had prepared for fire by installing cast-iron shutters on their buildings to halt the spread of flames. This precaution did no good; the heat from the fire following the earthquake simply melted the metal and made the shutters useless. But after the fire had burned itself out, having consumed venerable old St. Mary's Church and many other houses of worship, the Hotaling liquor warehouse could be seen still standing in the Barbary Coast. A song celebrated the warehouse's survival:

> *If, as they say, God spanked the town*
> *For being overfrisky,*
> *Why did He burn the churches down*
> *And spare Hotaling's whisky?*

Actually, no divine power was involved. The warehouse was saved by a team of brave sailors who ran a fire hose inland from the bay two miles away, to protect the building and its precious contents.

After the fire burned itself out, San Francisco looked much as Dresden did after Allied bombers did their work during World War II. Only a few large structures, such as the St. Francis Hotel, had survived both the fire and the earthquake. All around lay acre upon acre of ash and rubble. Iron fences stood in grotesque curlicue shapes where the heat of the flames had partially melted the metal. And downtown one could see an ironic tableau at the Donahue Fountain, where a monument to the spirit of industry—a giant bronze sculpture showing men straining to work a lever—stood in the midst of almost total destruction.

Far more monumental than the sculpture was the task that now faced Mayor Schmitz and General Funston. They had to restore order to a demolished city. Most of the population was homeless and destitute. San Franciscans needed food, clothing, and shelter. Emergency public health measures were needed to forestall epidemics; sewers had broken, running water was almost nonexistent, and cases of typhoid were already being reported.

Somehow all these massive efforts had to be coordinated effectively, despite the loss of telephone and wireless service. A few decades earlier, in the horse-and-buggy age, that task might have been impossible. But Funston had modern technology on his side, in the form of the automobile.

The general requisitioned all the private motorcars in San Francisco, along with their drivers, many of whom volunteered for duty. Funston's fleet of cars kept communication lines open in San Francisco in the days immediately following the quake and fire. At one point Funston had to turn his own front yard into a parking lot.

San Francisco under martial law was a sometimes perilous place to be. Vigilante groups roamed the city, dispensing their impromptu brand of "justice." Trigger-happy soldiers were another concern. One physician was shot dead by soldiers while running an errand in his automobile for General Funston. The soldiers thought he was stealing a car.

Draconian penalties were imposed for violating the military's edicts, especially where public health measures were concerned. One street sign pointed out, in no uncertain terms, that disobedience could be unhealthful in more ways than one:

SEWERS BLOCKED
Don't Use Toilets
Epidemic Threatened
OBEY ORDERS OR GET SHOT

But if the soldiers sometimes behaved like an occupying army (which, technically, they were), they also had the public interest at heart. They protected the homeless from profiteering grocers who thought they could use the earthquake as an excuse to charge astronomical prices. When one food merchant tried to charge a dollar a loaf for bread—twenty times the prequake rate—he found himself confronting a row of bayonets. The price went down.

Meanwhile, tent cities went up in the parks. Golden Gate Park looked like an army bivouac. The homeless who lacked tents found shelter as best they could, in lean-tos and hastily constructed shacks. Somehow San Franciscans maintained their sense of humor through it all and posted whimsical signs in front of their temporary homes. "Hotel de Bum," one read. Another urged simply, "Cheer up."

A month or so after the earthquake, a summary of the damage was available. The financial loss from the quake was estimated at half a billion dollars. Almost 500 blocks, or about 2,800 acres, of the city had been leveled by fire. Among the structures destroyed were 30 schools and 80 churches and convents. Approximately 250,000 men, women, and children—half the city's population—were left homeless. Some 30,000 buildings were destroyed (about 3,000 of those by the fire), and the initial estimate of deaths from the earthquake was 667: 315 bodies recovered plus 352 persons missing and unaccounted for. That estimate has risen to more than 2,000 today, and San Francisco's city archives office receives several letters every week containing information on victims of the earthquake.

Elder J. R. Shepard, the Mormon who had prayed for divine wrath to smite the city, was conscience-stricken after the earthquake. According to a 1983 article in the *Brigham Young University Journal*, Shepard had to be reassured that his prayer at the church social the previous night was not to blame for the catastrophe.

It is not quite accurate to refer to this quake as the "San Francisco earthquake," for San Francisco was only one of many communities affected. The earthquake caused extensive damage for more than 250 miles along the California coast. Santa Rosa, just north of San Francisco, was hit hardest by the earthquake; some seventy-five of its residents were killed, a proportion twenty times higher than in San Francisco. As in San Francisco, fire followed the quake in Santa Rosa, but the flames were brought under control before they reached the residential district. An eyewitness account of the damage described Santa Rosa as "a total wreck . . . the whole business portion tumbled into ruins. The main street is piled many feet deep with the fallen buildings. Not one business building . . . is left intact." Some of those who died in Santa Rosa were overcome by heat and smoke as they braved the fire to rescue valuables.

The south bay area was also devastated. In San Jose, the collapse of a mental institution killed 111 persons, and Stanford University in Palo Alto—where William James rode out the earthquake—lost most of its then new campus buildings.

As soon as they felt the earthquake, Stanford students rushed out of their dormitories into the open fields nearby. Encina Hall, a new four-story men's dormitory, was severely damaged when one of its chimneys collapsed and fell through all four floors to the basement, carrying six students along with it. Only two students were killed, but the remaining four sustained painful injuries. Amazingly, no one in the women's dormitories was hurt, "although many escapes were miraculous," one San Francisco paper reported.

Many another city would have needed a decade or more to recover from such losses, but San Franciscans started rebuilding almost immediately. Mark Twain, doubtless recalling his experiences in the earthquake of 1868, made a personal appeal for aid for San Francisco. Speaking to an audience at Carnegie Hall in New York City two days after the earthquake, Twain said, "I offer an appeal on behalf of that multitude, of that pathetic army of fathers, mothers, and children, sheltered and happy two days ago, now wandering hopeless, forlorn, and homeless, victims of immeasurable disaster. I say I beg of you in your heart . . . to remember San Francisco, the smitten city."

At a benefit in Chicago to aid a relief fund for San Franciscans, actress Sarah Bernhardt—who had donated a huge tent for the occasion—told the audience, "The calamity which has struck San Francisco has had an echo in the hearts of the people of the entire world. . . . Those who, like myself, have had the joy of visiting that admirable city have the feeling of a yet deeper sorrow. Nevertheless . . . like the phoenix, San Francisco will rise again from the ashes, greater, more beautiful, and stronger." When she finished, there was not one dry eye in the audience. The benefit raised more than $15,000, a hefty sum indeed in 1906. Twice that amount flowed in from another campaign in Chicago, where the mayor declared "San Francisco Day" and sent the city's policemen from door to door collecting funds for the San Franciscans.

Aided by contributions of food, medical supplies, tents for temporary housing, and cash totaling some $9 million, San Franciscans erected a whole new city on the ashes and rubble of the old. But not an entirely new city: though some visionary planners dreamed of a radically different design for the rebuilt San Francisco, the dream collapsed like a popped baloon in the face of economic realities.

Shortly before the earthquake and fire, a committee of civic-minded San Franciscans had called on the famous Chicago architect David Burnham to formulate a plan for beautifying their city. Burnham came up with a grand scheme. He wanted to rebuild San Francisco on the model of Paris, with broad boulevards and concentric ring roads centered on the waterfront to allow quick and easy access to all portions of the city.

In theory, Burnham's plan was just what San Francisco needed, and eventually many elements of his design were incorporated into U.S. city planning; but not in San Francisco. Too many buildings remained standing after the fire to make the Burnham plan practical. Moving those structures would have added tremendous expense to the already monumental cost of clearing away the debris and rebuilding all that was destroyed.

So the Burnham plan was shelved, and San Francisco after the quake and fire rose from the ashes more or less in its earlier form—but with some important differences. The reconstructed city had an extensive system of reservoirs, secondary water mains, and widely distributed cisterns to guarantee an adequate water supply to fight any future conflagration.

Three years after the earthquake, the city's real estate values had increased by 50 percent on the average, and San Francisco had most of the steel-frame buildings in the United States. It also had a cover-up in the making. Developers wanted to get rich from the rebuilding of San Francisco, and the last thing they desired was talk of earthquakes—mysterious, unpredictable disasters that could devastate a whole city without warning —scaring away investors, builders, and tenants. So when the local boosters spoke of the disaster of 1906, they were careful to describe it as "the San Francisco *fire* of 1906," with no mention at all of the earthquake.

This quiet understanding did much to stifle seismological research and public discussion of earthquake hazards in the Bay Area. Scientists were warned against investigating earthquakes and especially against talking about quakes in public. Andrew Lawson, the distinguished geologist who gave the San Andreas Fault its name, felt intense pressure from San Francisco's business community to avoid discussing the 1906 earthquake.

The businessmen were afraid of Lawson because of his outstanding work in analyzing the effects of the quake. At Lawson's suggestion, the state of California set up a commission to investigate the disaster and appointed Lawson to head the panel. With financial backing from Andrew Carnegie, Lawson's group produced a huge two-volume report entitled *The California Earthquake of 1906.*

Lawson's report was a model of scientific writing and became perhaps the single most famous work in the literature of geology. It also scared the business community of San Francisco because Lawson established the earthquake beyond all question as the cause of the 1906 calamity. The businessmen could not destroy his report, but they kept an eye on Lawson and put pressure on him to be quiet when, in 1911, he founded a national society for research on earthquakes and began publishing a journal on quake research.

Lawson refused to be silenced. On the contrary, he took on his critics in the first issue of his journal. "The commercial spirit of the people," he wrote, "fears any discussion of earthquakes, for the same reason that it [opposes] any mention of an occurrence of plague in the city of San Francisco." The business community believed, he went on, that discussion of earthquakes would hurt business.

In the end the businessmen won, and the San Francisco

media drew a curtain of silence around the entire subject of earthquakes. A reporter for one San Francisco newspaper, a few years after Lawson's journal started appearing, asked a geology professor at Stanford University about a mild quake that had shaken the city. The professor complied but added he was certain the paper would never print the reporter's copy. The professor was right; the story was killed. Thus the lessons of the 1906 earthquake were eventually forgotten.

March 10, 1910. A strong quake in the Monterey region was felt over an area of some sixty thousand square miles.

May 15, 1910. Coldwater Canyon was shaken violently, but there were no fatalities.

July 1, 1911. An intense earthquake struck the Santa Clara Valley around 2:00 P.M. The thirty-six-inch refracting telescope at Mount Hamilton Observatory shifted almost an inch on its base, and an adjacent brick dormitory was so badly damaged that it had to be torn down. This quake was also felt over an area of about sixty thousand square miles.

June 25, 1915. An earthquake in Imperial Valley caused large cracks to open in the ground. Six persons were crushed to death by falling walls in Mexicali.

October 22, 1916. An earthquake struck the Fort Tejon area. This tremor was not as violent as the 1857 event, but it cracked a concrete highway and knocked goods off shelves in stores. The quake was reportedly preceded by a noise like an approaching automobile.

April 21, 1918. A large quake shook San Jacinto. No one was killed, but only two buildings in the whole town were left standing. One newspaper report said the earthquake "started with a vertical bumping movement, then a twisting and rocking motion, with walls creaking and groaning, [and] windows rattling. . . . Doors opened and swayed back and forth."

June 29, 1925. The whole downtown business district of Santa Barbara was leveled by an earthquake, and a dam north of the city was destroyed. Some twenty persons were killed. This quake was remarkable for having a large number of aftershocks.

October 22, 1926. Two early morning earthquakes centered somewhere off the Monterey shore were felt over a hundred-thousand-square-mile area.

November 4, 1927. An earthquake near Lompoc generated a tsunami six feet high. The wave was detected later off San Francisco and San Diego.

March 10, 1933. One of California's most famous earthquakes, the Long Beach quake, occurred on this date. One hundred and twenty persons were reported killed, but the toll could easily have been much higher. The main shock occurred just before 6:00 P.M. Had it struck several hours earlier, thousands of children would probably have been killed in collapsing school buildings.

The earthquake was centered offshore, several miles southwest of Newport Beach. Drivers suddenly found their cars unmanageable, and to make matters worse, lampposts began falling in the streets. Gas tanks near Long Beach exploded, and a nearby transformer station "went out . . . with a dazzling pyrotechnic display," one eyewitness said.

Physicist Albert Einstein happened to be visiting the University of California in Long Beach that day, as the guest of a geologist on the faculty. Einstein wanted to know something about the science of earthquakes, and he walked through the campus with his host, discussing quake motions. Suddenly the two men noticed a commotion around them and saw students and faculty running out of campus buildings. The two scientists had been so intent on seismology that they had not noticed the earthquake taking place around them.

The Long Beach earthquake marked a turning point in Californians' attitudes toward earthquakes. Previously, Angelenos (evidently having forgotten the Fort Tejon event of 1857) presumed their part of California was relatively safe from destructive quakes. The Long Beach quake changed their minds in a hurry. It also changed California law: the destruction of several school buildings in Long Beach, and the narrow escape of their pupils, led the California legislature to pass the Field Act, which provided for improved building codes.

May 18, 1940. This quake was a revelation to geologists, for its ground ruptures showed the exact course of the Imperial Fault, of which we will see more later. The earthquake was centered near El Centro, just north of the Mexican border, and destroyed four-fifths of the buildings in the town of Imperial, California. Irrigation systems in local farmland were badly damaged, and the earthquake altered the border between the

United States and Mexico by shifting the position of the International Canal almost fifteen feet. Part of Baja California was flooded when another canal was ruptured by the quake. Though the main shock was brief—only about twelve seconds —it caused widespread damage. In Arizona's Yuma Valley, wells reportedly spewed water fifteen feet into the air.

July 21, 1952. The earthquake that struck Bakersfield on this date was the most powerful in California since the 1906 disaster in San Francisco and the strongest quake in southern California since the Fort Tejon event in 1857. Starting at 4:52 A.M., the earthquake was felt throughout southern California but was responsible for only a dozen fatalities, partly because so much of the area affected was sparsely populated. Four railroad tunnels collapsed, and Southern Pacific railway tracks near Bealville were warped. Damage to buildings was surprisingly light; destruction was confined largely to older structures made of adobe or brick. On the other hand, farms were hit hard by the quake, which knocked out irrigation systems and caused millions of dollars' worth of crop losses. The initial shock came without warning, but quake activity was slow to die down afterward; hundreds of aftershocks were reported in the following months. One of these, on August 22, was strong enough to kill two more persons and cause several million dollars in additional damage to Bakersfield.

October 23, 1955. An earthquake centered near Concord caused an estimated $1 million in property damage.

February 9, 1971. The San Fernando earthquake on this date will be the subject of a later chapter.

July 8, 1986. The most powerful earthquake in southern California in almost a decade struck at 2:21 A.M. at the edge of the Mojave Desert near Palm Springs, just east of Los Angeles. The quake shattered windows, touched off fires, and knocked out power. Vibrations from the earthquake were felt from Lake Havasu City, Arizona, to the San Fernando Valley north of Los Angeles. One fire that destroyed a glass shop in Palm Springs and caused $75,000 in damages was believed to have started when something ignited gas leaking from a pipe ruptured by the quake. Rock slides closed several highways in the desert, and a landslide cracked a bridge on Highway 111 near Palm Springs. There were no fatalities, and injuries were few: the Riverside County sheriff's office reported that one prisoner at a local minimum-security facility was so frightened that he jumped through a window, badly slashing a finger in the process. Area hospitals reported five persons were admitted complaining of chest pains caused by the earthquake, and ten persons were treated for sprained limbs after the quake shook them out of bed.

July 14, 1986. Less than a week after the Palm Springs quake of July 8, another earthquake rumbled through southern California. This quake struck shortly after dawn offshore near Oceanside and was felt along a 150-mile-long stretch of coastline between San Diego and Oxnard, northwest of Los Angeles. One person died of a heart attack during the earthquake.

Hundreds of earthquakes—most of them tiny but some perceptible to the unaided senses—shake California on any given day. Earthquakes are ten times more common in California than over the globe as an average. To understand just why quakes strike California so often, let us look back in time to see how California formed and how a rapidly moving sliver of rock created the conditions that put Californians in such peril today.

2

The How and Why of Earthquakes

On hearing the word *earthquake*, one usually thinks of a disaster scene on the Hollywood model, with buildings crumbling, dams collapsing, and terrified people running screaming into the streets. Though some earthquakes fit that description, most do not. Many quakes are brief but imperceptible, while others occur in "slow motion," so that only the most sensitive recording instruments can tell that the earth has moved at all.

Earthquakes are notoriously unpredictable. Some occur in active earthquake zones, and others turn up where they are least expected—in normally tranquil spots where earthquakes ought to be as rare as dragons. And though earthquakes are among the most familiar phenomena of nature, they are also among the most mysterious and poorly understood.

Since an impending earthquake is the subject of this book, we should devote a chapter to the phenomenon of earthquakes: what they are, what causes them, and how they have given us a window, so to speak, into the mysterious interior of our planet. Then we can better understand why California is known as "earthquake country" and why earthquakes there pose hazards unique to the state.

An earthquake may be broadly defined as any measurable

EPICENTER

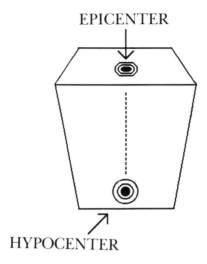

HYPOCENTER

Hypocenter vs. Epicenter: The *hypocenter*, or focus, of an earthquake is the point underground where the disturbance is centered. The *epicenter* is the point on the surface directly above the hypocenter. *(Courtesy of Allan Frank)*

vibration of the earth's surface. The technical term for an earthquake is *temblor* or *seismic event*.

Earthquakes, some geologists are fond of saying, are like crimes. Each one is unique, and every one has a special set of precipitating factors. Quakes may be set off by any of several dozen different "triggers," from cold weather to atomic bomb tests to the slow but relentless movements of the earth itself.

Although an earthquake may occur almost anywhere on earth, most take place place along faults, cracks in the earth's surface along which masses of rock move relative to each other. When that movement is not smooth, the rock masses tend to stick together, and strain builds up. The sudden release of that strain results in an earthquake.

When a quake occurs, its point of origin underground is called the *hypocenter* or *focus*. The hypocenter should not be confused with the more familiar expression *epicenter*, meaning the point on the surface directly above the hypocenter.

An earthquake generates several kinds of waves in the rocks of the earth. Only two of these are important to us here: *S-waves* and *P-waves*.

The "S" in S-waves stands for several things. One is *surface*.

S-waves ripple out along the surface from the origin of the quake, just as ripples spread out over a pond when one drops in a stone. "S" also stands for *sinusoidal*, because S-waves seen in profile follow the familiar up-and-down pattern of sine waves. You can generate an artificial S-wave yourself by holding one end of a clothesline and shaking it up and down. Sinusoidal S-waves will ripple along the cord. In some cases, the S-wave from an earthquake can be seen with the unaided eye: remember, from the previous chapter, how a policeman in San Francisco saw the S-wave from the 1906 quake moving down the street toward him.

Finally, the "S" stands for *shear*. Shear is defined as motion at right angles to the direction in which the wave is advancing. In practical terms, shear is the shaking force, up and down or side to side, that results when the S-waves pass. Shear from S-waves is what knocks down buildings, topples chimneys, and generally causes the havoc that one associates with major quakes. (Because S-waves produce ground motion at right angles—that is, transverse—to their direction of motion, they are sometimes called *transverse waves.*)

S-waves include one of the most colorfully named phenomena in geology: Love waves, designated after the physicist A. E. H. Love, who first analyzed them. When a Love wave passes, the ground moves back and forth horizontally. Another kind of S-wave is the Raleigh wave, first identified by the British scientist Lord Raleigh. A Raleigh wave behaves very much like a wave in the ocean. Particles caught in a Raleigh wave move up and down in an elliptical path as the wave goes by, but their net motion remains zero.

The force of S-waves is commonly measured in *g units.* One g stands for the normal force of gravity at sea level. A fast start in your car subjects you to perhaps half an extra g. Astronauts riding into orbit on the space shuttle experience about four g's during their ascent. An added g or two does the average person no harm. But as we will see later, even a fraction of an additional *g* from an earthquake's S-waves can prove lethal to buildings and the people inside them.

For all their destructive potential, S-waves typically are small. The S-wave that demolishes a home or factory may have an amplitude (half the distance from crest to trough) of only four inches—no higher than a kitten's shoulder. It takes a truly colossal event of nature, such as a giant meteorite impact, to generate S-waves more than a foot or two high. Most human-built structures are so delicately balanced, however, that even an S-wave three or four inches high can bring them tumbling down.

More difficult to see, but just as important to seismologists, are the P-waves, or pressure waves. These travel deep into the earth, penetrating in some cases all the way through the planet.

P-waves are not sinusoidal ripples, as S-waves are. P-waves represent a moving, compressional shock front of energy traveling from particle to particle through the rocks. In college geology courses, instructors demonstrate the physics of P-waves with the aid of an ordinary brass-wire spring. Hang the spring from the ceiling and jiggle the free end up and down. Compressional waves will ripple along the spring as the coils come together and then move apart. What you see is a P-wave much like those generated by an earthquake.

P-waves are commonly detected thousands of miles away from the site of a major earthquake, and their global range has made them a godsend to geophysicists. By analyzing the velocities of P-waves traveling through the earth's interior, scientists have been able to piece together a detailed picture of the earth's "entrails." This picture will be discussed in detail later; for now it suffices to say that the interior of the earth, far from being the simple system it was once believed to be, is looking more complex all the time.

Earthquake waves are measured using instruments called *seismographs*. The first modern seismographs were developed in the late nineteenth century and made it possible, for the first time, to record on paper (or, in early models, on rotating smoked drums) the vibrations of an earthquake. When put down on paper, this record is called a *seismogram*. It registers time measured in seconds on the horizontal axis and ground motion measured in millimeters on the vertical axis. Nowadays a seismograph is more likely to record the earthquake data on magnetic tape. The seismograph must not only detect quake vibrations, but amplify them as well so that they are easier to record. In some cases, amplification of five thousand times or more is necessary to produce a legible recording.

The heart of a seismograph, so to speak, is a component called the *seismometer*. It may be a pendulum or a block of some heavy material mounted on a spring. The seismometer sways or jiggles in response to earthquake vibrations, and its motion is transferred to the recording apparatus.

How much destruction an earthquake causes depends on many different factors, including:

• *Magnitude.* This means how much energy is released in the earthquake. Magnitude is not necessarily synonymous with damage; a powerful quake may do only minimal damage to persons and property, while a relatively minor quake can be much more devastating under the proper conditions.

Determining the energy of an earthquake is tricky because so much energy is released over such a wide area. The most commonly used scales of quake magnitude are the Richter and Mercalli scales. Each uses a different set of criteria to fix the intensity of a quake.

The Richter scale is named after Dr. Charles Richter, a geologist at the California Institute of Technology. He proposed the scale in a paper published in 1935. It is a simple logarithmic scale—that is, expressed in powers of 10—that records the intensity of ground movement as measured in microns, tiny metric units of distance. (One inch equals about 26,000 microns.)

Geologists measuring a quake on the Richter scale do not simply look at a measuring device and read off a magnitude figure. Determining a quake's place on the Richter scale is much more complicated than that.

When instruments start picking up the vibrations from an earthquake, scientists first have to figure where the quake is centered. This is fairly easy. Note the direction of the waves as they pass two widely separated locations, and one can locate the epicenter by recording the waves' time of arrival at each station and plugging the data into a set of equations that determines the distance from each station to the focus of the temblor.

Now things get trickier, because of a property of earthquake waves. They get weaker as they ripple out from the focus of the quake, so an earthquake that seems strong to someone standing on the epicenter may feel comparatively mild to another person perhaps a hundred miles away. How, then, can one arrive at a single magnitude figure, when the quake's effects vary so much with distance?

Richter attacked that problem by setting a standard distance for the measurements. The Richter scale expresses the magnitude of a quake as measured one hundred kilometers (a little over sixty miles) from the focus.

Unfortunately quakes seldom occur precisely one hundred kilometers from measuring devices, so one has to use a correction factor to determine what the ground movement would be at one hundred kilometers from the focus. But the correction factors introduce some error into the process. That is why observers in two different locations, miles apart, may come up with different Richter magnitudes for a given earthquake.

To make things even more confusing, the instruments used at one site may behave differently from those at another location. Depending on what kind of instruments you use, you may have to apply yet another correction factor.

So the Richter scale is not a completely acccurate measure of an earthquake's strength. Nonetheless, it provides a simple and —within certain limits—reliable estimate of the energy released in an earthquake.

The Richter scale starts at zero and is open-ended. It bears some resemblance to the scale of magnitude used to measure the brightness of stars; this is not coincidence, since Richter was an amateur astronomer and borrowed the expression "magnitude" from that brightness classification. Richter did not, incidentally, name the scale after himself. A self-effacing man, he actually refused to call it the Richter scale in his writings.

The popular success of his invention sometimes caused unpleasantness for Richter. After the Richter scale became famous, he was pestered by curious souls who thought he had built some marvelous quake-measuring machine, not a mere mathematical scale of magnitude. "Every year they come by, wanting to look at my scale," Richter once said in a newspaper interview.

Richter's scale is convenient for scientists who have access to sophisticated equipment. But suppose you are standing on the sidewalk when an earthquake hits. You have no way to measure the amplitude of S-waves in microns. How can you figure the intensity of the quake under those circumstances?

Fortunately another scale—less precise, but easier to use—is available. It was developed by the Italian geologist Giuseppe Mercalli in 1902 and uses on-the-spot observations of a quake's effects to determine how strong the earthquake is. The Mercalli scale is highly detailed and describes practically anything that can happen in an earthquake, in levels of intensity ranging from I to XII. (Mercalli's scale uses roman numerals to avoid confusion with Richter magnitudes.) Here is a brief summary of the Mercalli scale:

MERCALLI INTENSITY	OBSERVED EFFECTS
I	Not felt at all.
II	Felt only by a few individuals, indoors and at rest, usually on upper floors of tall buildings.
III	Felt indoors by many persons, but not necessarily recognized as an earthquake. Chandeliers and hanging plants swing.
IV	Felt both indoors and out. Feels like the vibration caused by a heavy truck or train passing. Windows rattle.
V	Strong enough to awaken sleeping persons. Small objects knocked off shelves. Beverages may splash out of cups or glasses on tables.
VI	Perceptible to everyone. May cause public fright. Pictures fall off walls. Weak masonry cracks. Some plaster may fall from ceilings.
VII	Difficult to stand upright. Ornamental masonry falls from buildings. Waves may be seen in ponds and swimming pools.
VIII	Mass panic may occur. Chimneys, smokestacks, and water towers may lean and fall. Unsecured frame houses slide off foundations.
IX	Panic is general. Heavy damage to masonry structures and to underground pipes. Large cracks open in ground.
X	Many buildings collapse. Water splashes over riverbanks.
XI–XII	Virtually total destruction.

How powerful an earthquake can be no one knows. That is why the Richter scale is open-ended. Most scientists presume there is some upper limit on earthquake magnitude—probably near Richter magnitude 9.0—simply because the strength of the materials of the earth, and the forces at work on them, are finite, though tremendous. But there is no way of telling exactly where the upper limit of quake magnitude lies. In theory, earthquakes of magnitude 10 or 11 are possible, but only the most extraordinary conditions (say, the collision of a giant meteorite with the earth) could give rise to temblors of such magnitudes.

The two strongest earthquakes ever recorded, one under the Pacific Ocean near Japan in 1933 and the other off the coast of Ecuador in 1906, had a magnitude of roughly 8.9. The San Francisco disaster of 1906 is believed to have measured about 8.2 on the Richter scale (XII on the Mercalli scale), while the most powerful earthquakes in U.S. history—the New Madrid, Missouri, quakes of 1811 and 1812—are estimated at about 8.6. Neither the Richter scale nor reliable quake-recording instruments had been invented at that time, so the 8.6 figure is really just an educated guess. Though the New Madrid quakes were probably much greater in magnitude than the San Francisco earthquake a century later, the Missouri earthquakes did much less damage because the area was sparsely settled then. Population density also is an important influence on earthquake damage. A densely settled area is clearly more susceptible to harm than a wilderness.

Several other factors bear on an earthquake's effects:

• *Duration.* Some quakes are over within five seconds; others may last two minutes or more. Generally speaking, the longer a quake, the more damage it will do.

• *Local geology.* The nature of underlying material can make the difference between survival and complete destruction for a community caught in an earthquake. In 1906 San Franciscans learned to their dismay that it was unsafe to build on landfill or any other poorly consolidated material. It lost cohesion as the earthquake shook the soil, so the buildings atop the landfill suddenly were unsupported and collapsed. This effect is called *liquefaction,* and it occurs when passing S-waves suddenly raise the pressure of groundwater in pores between soil grains. The soil liquefies, and any structure on top of the suddenly soupy soil is liable to sink into it like a torpedoed ship. We will discuss liquefaction at length in a later discussion of the geology of the Los Angeles area.

Local geology also determines how far a quake will be felt. Some materials and geological structures act as earthquake "dampers," dissipating S-waves and confining destruction to a reasonable area. But under other conditions the shock from an earthquake may be felt strongly a thousand miles or more from its point of origin. The 1906 San Francisco earthquake, for example, was barely felt at all east of the Rockies, because the rocks in the mountains had been twisted and broken up by the mountain-building process. The fractured rocks acted as a giant shock absorber, soaking up the energy from the earthquake. In the East, however, conditions are very different. Over large stretches of the eastern United States, there are no "dampers" to absorb S- and P-waves, so the shock from an earthquake may be perceptible a thousand miles away from the epicenter. Later, we will deal with this effect at greater length, in connection with an earthquake hazard facing the Midwest.

• *Time of day.* This factor does more than perhaps any other to determine the number of casualties from a quake. More people are likely to be killed in collapsing buildings if an earthquake strikes around breakfast time, when nearly everyone is still indoors, than at midmorning, when most people are out of the house. A 1983 earthquake in Coalinga, California, for example, destroyed the downtown area but was relatively sparing of life, because most townspeople were at home when the quake occurred—not on the downtown streets, where they could have been killed or injured by collapsing buildings or falling debris.

• *Building construction.* Some kinds of architecture, either by accident or design, are much more quake-resistant than others. Adobe, for example, is perhaps the worst material to use in an earthquake-prone area; reinforced concrete is better. But for many purposes, the most quakeproof kind of building is the traditional American single wood-frame house. Its wooden construction makes it more resilient than rigid brick or stone and therefore more likely to survive the ravages of S-waves. The Japanese, who live in the most quake-ridden land of all, learned this trick of architecture centuries ago. Traditional Japanese homes, before the twentieth century, at least, were constructed largely of wood and paper: materials well suited to

surviving the stresses of earthquakes and much easier to replace than brick or stone in the event a house was destroyed.

As perhaps the most dramatic events of nature, earthquakes
helped to give the earth sciences their start. Chinese scholars
were studying earthquakes with primitive quake-recording instruments as early as the first century B.C.

China's first professional seismologist was a savant named
Choko, who devised the world's earliest seismometer. It consisted of a large brass tub with eight metal dragon figures
mounted equidistantly around it. Each dragon held a ball in its
mouth. If the vibrations from an earthquake jiggled the tub,
the dragon facing in the direction of their origin would drop
its ball into the open mouth of a brass frog waiting below.

Choko's colleagues (the story goes) were skeptical about his
invention and grew even more so when one of the dragons was
found to have released the ball from its mouth, though no one
had felt an earthquake. Choko was vindicated, however, when
news arrived several days later about a great earthquake that
had shaken a province several hundred miles away, just when
Choko's invention had registered a seismic disturbance. Moreover, the dragon that dropped its ball was pointing straight
toward the focus of the earthquake.

Suddenly Choko's critics were converted, and he was hailed
as a genius. Even the emperor was impressed and made Choko
the nation's official seismologist. No one, except possibly
Choko, knew his success was due to pure luck. His device was
not nearly sensitive enough to pinpoint the foci of earthquakes
so precisely. It was sheerest chance that his primitive seismometer had indicated the correct direction.

The Chinese have had plenty of opportunity to learn about
earthquakes, for their land has been shaken by mighty seismic
events every few decades for more than four thousand years.
Among the earliest records passed down to us from ancient
China is a report of an earthquake that killed some eight
hundred thousand persons. (Such casualty figures should be
viewed with skepticism because they tend to be inflated in the
telling and retelling over hundreds of years.)

But seismology did not progress very far in imperial China,
partly because of the peculiar Chinese attitude toward phenomena of nature. Unlike Western scholars, who believed in a

mechanistic, clockwork universe where everything was governed by physical laws that humans could figure out and utilize as tools, the Chinese ascribed most natural phenomena to the work of spirits. Just about everything in Chinese experience had its own special demon, god, or other spirit assigned to it. Among the deities responsible for earthquakes was Mo-li Hung, one of the so-called diamond kings of heaven, four celestial brothers who used their supernatural powers to reward the righteous and chastise evildoers. Mo-li Hung's name translates roughly as "bringer of huge events." His principal weapon was the Umbrella of Chaos, made of magical pearls. When Mo-li Hung opened his umbrella, the Chinese believed, earthquakes shook the world, and violent storms arose.

Such legends made for colorful lore but did little to encourage scientific study of earthquakes. Who, after all, wanted to risk disaster by poking around in the professional business of a diamond king of heaven? So it remained for the Europeans to pioneer seismology.

Aristotle, whose writings stood as the final word in matters of natural history for more than a thousand years in Europe, came up with an imaginative but inaccurate theory of how earthquakes occur. He surmised that when the weather was still and hot, air made its way from the surface into deep underground caverns, where it was heated by the underground fires that produced volcanoes. Now and then, Aristotle suggested, air pressure underground built up to such intensity that the superheated gas burst out through the surface, causing earthquakes and volcanic eruptions. Aristotle's conjecture is the reason that warm, windless conditions came to be known as "earthquake weather."

This model of quake activity may seem quaint today, but in Aristotle's time it seemed reasonable. Scholars then had no way of knowing that the earth's interior is solid, not honeycombed with subterranean passages full of hot air. (Indeed, belief in a spongy-textured earth, honeycombed throughout with caverns, persisted well into the nineteenth century and inspired some entertaining fiction, notably Jules Verne's still popular novel *Journey to the Center of the Earth*.) Also, volcanoes give off great outbursts of gas when they erupt, and since earthquakes are often associated with volcanic activity, Aristotle probably had good reason to think quakes and eruptions were powered by superheated air escaping from underground. Four centuries after Aristotle, the famous naturalist Pliny the Elder, a credulous collector of tall stories, backed Aristotle's model of quake activity when he wrote: "Tremors of the earth . . . occur [only] when the seas are calm and the air so still that birds cannot fly."

In Europe, the ancient Greek philosophers were among the earliest seismologists, or scientists who study earthquakes. The Greeks lived in a quake-prone land (the Mediterranean basin is one of the most seismically active parts of the world), but they, like modern scientists, were handicapped in their studies by the fact that it is difficult to experiment with earthquakes. Quakes happen so unexpectedly that it was hard for the Greeks to study earth tremors while quakes were under way. Only by studying their descriptions and effects could ancient philosophers try to determine what instigates earthquakes. Understandably, then, some of their hypotheses were misguided. About 600 B.C., the philosopher Thales suggested that earthquakes were caused by powerful waves striking the shore; but this explanation did not account for the many earthquakes that occur far inland. Anaximenes, who lived about a century after Thales, thought earthquakes might be the vibrations caused by great chunks of rock falling from the roofs of underground caverns. He was on the right track—many earthquakes do result from the collision of masses of subterranean rock—but this hypothesis, too, proved untenable. Archelaus proposed that earthquakes happened when highly compressed gas escaped from deep underground. This, modern geologists think, was a prescient view of the cause of earthquakes; as we will see later, many geologists today think earthquakes are often accompanied by a release of gas that has been trapped inside the earth since its formation and is only now seeping to the surface.

For almost 2,500 years after Thales and company speculated on the origins of earthquakes, scholars made little progress in understanding what makes the earth shake. Yet data kept accumulating on the magnitudes, dates, and locations of earthquakes, and by the mid-1800s the time was right for an Irish engineer named Robert Mallet to fit the data into a global pattern.

Earthquakes were Mallet's avocation. Though he was a gifted and successful engineer (some of the bridges and railway stations he designed are still standing in Britain), he is best remembered for a report he published about an earthquake in Italy. Titled *The Great Neapolitan Earthquake of 1857,* Mallet's book went down in history as a classic of scientific reporting, and his meticulous observations of the quake's effects set the standard for future seismologists.

Mallet also made a smaller but more important contribution to seismology by drawing an earthquake map of the world. He plotted the locations of all reliably recorded earthquakes in historical records, and the result was a strange-looking chart indeed to nineteenth-century eyes.

Mallet's map showed that earthquakes were not distributed evenly over the globe, as one might expect, but instead were concentrated in a handful of curved belts that encircled the world like the seams on a soccer ball or the netting around a fisherman's glass float. The Caribbean Sea showed up clearly on Mallet's map as a hotbed of seismicity. Across the Atlantic, a dark band of earthquake activity ran east from Spain and Portugal across the Mediterranean basin, through Persia (now Iran) and Afghanistan, and along the towering Himalaya mountain chain between China and India. Along the western shore of the Pacific Ocean was another concentration of earthquakes; Mallet drew a dark band of quake potential through Japan, the Philippines, and the eastern shore of China.

The western Pacific earthquake zone on Mallet's map looked like a parenthesis mark half enclosing the ocean. The second "parenthesis" in the Pacific set was a band of earthquake activity running down the Pacific shores of the Americas, from Alaska in the north to Tierra del Fuego in the south. Together, these two circum-Pacific belts of unstable ground are known informally as the "ring of fire" and contain three-fourths of all the earthquake and volcanic activity on earth.

Mallet's global earthquake map represented a quantum leap forward in the understanding of the earth we live on. But although his chart showed where earthquakes were concentrated, it did not explain why they followed this pattern of distribution. Indeed, Mallet's work raised as many questions as it answered.

For example, Mallet's earthquake belts tended to follow seashores, such as those of the Mediterranean and Pacific. Did that mean some link existed, as Thales had imagined centuries earlier, between earthquakes and the oceans? Not necessarily; Mallet's map also showed an intense concentration of quakes in the Himalayas, hundreds of miles from the nearest sea. The global distribution of earthquakes would baffle geologists for years after Mallet published his work.

But the patterns on Mallet's map did not remain a puzzle for long. Around the turn of the century, a solution was put forward by the least likely person imaginable: a German weatherman and adventurer with no formal training in geology.

His name was Alfred Wegener. Today he is revered as one of the secular saints of science for having put Mallet's data into proper perspective and, in doing so, laying the foundations for modern geology. Wegener was a colorful figure, and numerous myths have sprung up around his persona and his work. This is a good time to dispose of some of them.

Wegener was born in Berlin in 1880, the son of an evangelical minister. The young Wegener studied at the University of Heidelberg and at Berlin University, where he went to earn a doctorate in astronomy. Meterology seemed a more promising career than astronomy, however, and Wegener became a weatherman.

The early twentieth century was a fascinating time to be a meteorologist because scientists were developing a global model of atmospheric circulation, just as Mallet had done with earthquakes in the previous century. Moreover, the upper atmosphere—heretofore a realm of mystery—was yielding its secrets to high-altitude balloons and kites, and scientists were discovering that the thin upper air was a realm quite unlike the comparatively dense "weather layer" near the ground.

Most intriguing of all, from Wegener's viewpoint, was the role of the Arctic in generating weather systems. The frigid air of the Arctic is a weather factory, so to speak, for the Northern Hemisphere. As masses of cold air sweep southward from the Arctic, they collide with warmer air to the south and create the frontal systems familiar to watchers of the evening news today.

The Arctic's role in weather systems fascinated Wegener partly because he was already obsessed with one particular corner of the Arctic: Greenland, the vast snow-covered island between northern Europe and Canada. In hopes of visiting Greenland someday, Wegener put himself through a grueling regimen of training in Arctic sports, including cross-country skiing. His preparations paid off: in 1906 he was chosen to accompany a Danish meteorological expedition to Greenland. Wegener stayed in Greenland for two years, then returned to Germany, where he joined the faculty of Marburg University to teach meteorology. He also married Ilse Köppen, daughter of Vladimir Köppen, the most famous meteorologist of his day. The marriage was a good one, and Wegener, like Darwin and Freud before him, used the security and tranquility of a happy domestic life to incubate a revolutionary theory.

In his spare time, Wegener turned his attention from the atmospheric sciences to geology. The earth sciences then were much more tradition-bound than they are today, partly because an age-old and misguided belief had not yet fully released its grip on geologists' thinking.

Geologists in the first two decades of the twentieth century were still under the influence of an ancient school of scientific thought called *diluvianism.* It originated with the biblical story of Noah's Flood, which for centuries was taken as literal truth even by the most eminent scientists. (Isaac Newton, for example, seems to have accepted it unquestioningly.) According to diluvianism, the major features of our globe, such as the continents and ocean basins, were relics of a great ancient deluge and were supposed to have remained essentially unchanged since ancient times.

Of course scientists of the early 1900s no longer looked to the Bible for answers to questions of science, because most of the tenets of diluvianism had been discredited many years earlier, about the time Mallet was writing his book on the Neapolitan earthquake. But the central tradition of diluvianist thought, namely an ancient and essentially static earth, lingered in scientific thought past 1900 and made many geologists unwilling to harbor the thought that the solid earth might be a dynamic, ever-changing system like the atmosphere.

The essentials of the earth's internal structure had been worked out by 1900. Geologists knew the earth was divided into three parts:

- a heavy, iron-rich *core*
- a surrounding *mantle* that was made up of less dense rock and accounted for most of the earth's volume and mass
- a thin outer layer of lightweight rock called the *crust*

Scientists knew that the crust "floated" atop the denser rocks of the mantle, much as ice floes float on water. This floating effect is called *isostasy.* It was also clear that the crust had been fractured, upthrust, depressed, and generally tortured in numerous ways over the millions of years since its formation. Mountain ranges, for example, had been pushed up where seas had rolled only a few million years before. One dramatic piece of evidence to this effect was the geology of the Himalayas. Much of Mount Everest, the tallest peak on earth, is marine limestone that once formed part of a seabed.

The geology of Mount Everest was explained by invoking changes in sea level and crustal isostasy. To geologists of the early 1900s, it looked as if the sea once had covered the present site of the Himalayas long enough for marine limestone to form; then the waters retreated, and the change in isostasy— that is, an increase in "buoyancy" of the crustal rock—allowed the earth to rear up and form the mountains where earlier there had been a sea.

But this explanation was at odds with the structural geology of the mountains. The layers, or *strata,* of rock were not lying flat and parallel to the ground, as one might expect if a chunk of rock had just been lifted vertically from an ancient seabed. On the contrary, the strata were twisted, warped, and jumbled together in chaotic patterns. How could a mere uplift of land accomplish such havoc?

Turn-of-the-century geologists had an answer for that question, too. They figured that the earth originally had cooled, and was still cooling, from a molten to a solid state. As a rule, solid objects shrink as they cool. So geologists pointed to the chilling of the earth as a cause of mountain building. As the earth cooled down from its initial molten state, they reasoned, its diameter shrank, and the shrinkage caused crustal rocks to wrinkle and buckle upward in places. The result: mountain ranges.

That explanation seemed sound, in theory. But there was also a vexing problem with the global distribution of fossils.

Paleontologists—experts on fossils—commonly found the fossilized remains of a certain plant or animal species at widely separated points around the globe. One African dinosaur, for example, turned up fossilized in the rocks of South America, thousands of miles away. If the two continents had stayed immobile relative to each other since the days of the dinosaurs, how did those identical fossils come to lie on opposite sides of the Atlantic Ocean? No one seriously believed that identical species could have evolved independently of each other, on either side of the sea. But how could such realities be reconciled with the concept of a basically static, rigid crust?

Geologists tried. They invoked *land bridges*—strips of dry land between the continents, uncovered and then closed again by changes in isostasy to account for some far-flung fossils. Supposedly the dinosaurs, or whatever, marched from one continent to another when a land bridge existed, then were stranded when the land bridge disappeared under the seas.

But there were problems with this explanation. It required huge chunks of the earth's crust to bob up and down isostatically in much the same way submarines dive or surface by respectively filling or emptying their ballast tanks. A block of crust, however, had no "tanks" to blow or fill, so there was no known way for the rock to make itself more or less buoyant. Also, the land bridge in some instances would have had to be implausibly long (five thousand miles or more) or would have carried animals crossing the bridge into climates grossly unsuited to them. Yet there the fossils were, as out of place as hippos at the North Pole.

What was going on? Was the classical model of a rigid, motionless crust flawed? Could the continents have rearranged themselves somehow over geological time? And if they did so, then how? Those questions haunted geologists from the mid-1800s until after World War I, when Wegener's work forced a reexamination of three-hundred-year-old evidence.

For some three centuries before Wegener's day, scientists had been edging up to the notion that continents might move horizontally as well as vertically, sliding together and then drifting apart again. In 1620, the English scholar Francis Bacon looked at a map of the Atlantic and noticed how the outlines of the continents on either side of the ocean seemed to match, like pieces of a jigsaw puzzle. But Bacon did not deduce from that observation that the continents had once been joined into a single landmass that had broken apart.

Some wild ideas were put forward in the centuries after Bacon to account for the odd symmetry between the East and West coasts of the Atlantic. For example, the enduring fascination with the Atlantis legend stems in part from nineteenth-century books that invoked the destruction of that mythical landmass to explain the symmetrical pattern of the continents on either side of the ocean. (Prominent among America's nineteenth-century Atlantis cultists was Ignatius Donnelly, a novelist and one-time Populist candidate for president, who did much to publicize the Atlantis myth in his best-selling books.)

Reputable scientists dismissed such myths as nonsense. Yet those same scientists had a hard time throwing off the equally groundless, biblically rooted influence of diluvianism. When geologist Antonio Snider-Pelligrini proposed in 1858 that the continents might have moved horizontally, the only mechanism he could suggest for their motion was Noah's Flood.

Solid evidence for continental migration kept piling up during the late nineteenth century, however, thanks largely to the efforts of an Austrian geologist named Edward Suess, who gathered voluminous records of geological formations around the world, and an American named Frank Taylor.

A Harvard dropout, Taylor had rich parents and used part of their wealth to finance his own research expeditions into the geology of North America. For more than twenty years he toured the continent, gathering data on the structural and historical geology of the United States and Canada. In 1908 he published a paper called "The Bearing of the Tertiary Mountain Belt Upon the Earth's Plan," in which he suggested that some of North America's mountain ranges had been thrust up as the continent slid sideways over the surface of the earth. But Taylor was not a great popularizer of science, and his paper sat almost forgotten in libraries until it came to the attention of Alfred Wegener.

Between 1903 and 1910, Wegener took an interest in the idea of continental displacement. According to a widely told story, Wegener was seated on a costal hillside one day, watching ice floes drifting across the sea below, when he suddenly realized that the continents might be drifting as the ice floes were.

This anecdote is probably apocryphal. Wegener appears to have come across the drifting-continent hypothesis in the writings of Taylor and a British colliery manager named Pickering, who had written a paper trying to account for the birth of the Pacific Ocean basin. Wegener proceeded to flesh out the continental-displacement hypothesis with data from Suess's writings, and in 1912 Wegener's ideas appeared in print in an article for the *Marburg University Science Journal*. In 1915, after a brief career as an army officer (he served with distinction and was wounded twice), he published an expanded version of his theory in a book entitled *The Origins of Continents and Oceans*. In brief, this is what Wegener said:

The continents are not fixed in position but instead are sliding slowly about the face of the earth. Once, the continents we recognize today were all joined together in a single giant landmass that Wegener called *Pangaea* (pronounced "pan-*jee*-ah"), meaning "all land." That supercontinent broke apart millions of years ago, and its fragments drifted eventually into their present locations. The breakup of Pangaea formed the Atlantic Ocean basin, and the westward motion of the Americas pushed up high mountains at their western, leading edges, where the continental crust was crumpled and uplifted by the continents' march across the globe.

Not everyone agreed with Wegener's ideas. They contradicted traditions that the scientific establishment had a professional interest in preserving. As one speaker pointed out at a meeting of petroleum geologists in 1928, "If we are to believe Wegener's hypothesis, we must forget everything that has been learned in the past seventy years and start again." That was not a pleasant prospect for geologists who had earned their doctorates and built their reputations according to the old school of thought.

So Wegener's work was severely criticized. Sometimes his critics were unfair, but sometimes they had good reason for doubt. For example, Wegener based some of his speculations on incorrect or incomplete data. Faulty measurements led him to believe that Greenland was sliding westward at a rate of approximately a mile per year, when the correct figure is only about half an inch.

Wegener also showed a poor grasp of historical geology. At one point he claimed that the opening of the Atlantic, some one hundred million years ago on Wegener's time scale, was the same event that raised the Rocky Mountains in North America, only one hundred thousand years ago by his reckoning. Such blunders hurt Wegener's credibility and caused many traditional geologists to dismiss him as a crank or an inept amateur. Anti-German sentiment following World War I may also have worked against Wegener. In many circles during postwar years there was a tendency to regard any ideas emanating from Germany as the ravings of "the beastly Hun."

Some of Wegener's more worshipful biographers have portrayed him, in the years following publication of his theory, as a friendless outcast hounded by ignorant and cruel colleagues who were determined to suppress the great truth he had revealed. That image of Wegener is false. Wegener was not lynched by his fellow scientists. On the contrary, his converts soon outnumbered his critics. Science works in such a way that any reasonably sound new theory is bound to win some influential friends because it explains the previously inexplicable; and Wegener's work cleared up so many riddles of geology that he quickly acquired many defenders in the scientific community.

Wegener accounted for the sometimes puzzling global distribution of fossils, noted earlier. That pattern was easy to understand if one assumed that the fossils had originally been deposited in a single location on an ancient supercontinent, then dispersed when the giant landmass broke up. This was a much more reasonable mechanism than isostatic land bridges, which could never have behaved as traditionalists thought they did.

Still, conservatives among scientists refused to give Wegener's work their blessing until some weak spots in his theory were resolved. For instance, Wegener proposed that a "flight from the poles," or *Polflucht,* supplied the energy that moved the continents around. Wegener thought the centrifugal motion of the earth spinning on its axis was making the continents move toward the equator.

Isaac Newton had demonstrated this effect mathematically three centuries earlier, in his *Principia,* using two hypothetical columns of water—one drilled to the earth's center from the North Pole, the other from the equator, and both of equal length—to show that the earth's rotation caused an equatorward "pull" of sorts. Water in the column on the equator, Newton demonstrated, would rise slightly higher than water in the column drilled from the pole.

But Newton's math also showed that this effect was very slight. The difference between the two water levels would be a few inches at most. Was this enough to send the continents slipping toward the tropics, as Wegener postulated? Surely not. Thus Wegener effectively failed to explain what might be moving the continents around.

A more fundamental problem for some traditionalists was Wegener's assumption about the behavior of the solid earth. His theory called for rock far underground to flow almost like taffy if the continents were to move across the earth's surface as he suggested. Geologists knew that molten rock from volcanoes behaves as a fluid, and sometimes flows nearly as fast as water. But rock confined miles below the surface, under terrific pressure, was another matter entirely. Under those conditions rock would take on the properties of steel, not taffy. That fact led one of Wegener's leading critics, the British geologist Sir Harold Jeffreys, to deny flatly that the physical properties of the inner earth would permit the continents to move as Wegener imagined they did.

Jeffreys had a point. Wegener did seem to be trying to have it both ways, arguing that rock could be simultaneously rigid, like steel, and fluid, like molasses. But Canadian researchers resolved this seeming dilemma when they put samples of granite in a special testing device and found that the rock could indeed be deformed under great pressure—that is, made to flow—to a degree consistent with the needs of Wegener's theory. The rock did not have to flow very fast; a tiny fraction of an inch per day would do. So underground rock might seem as solid as Gibraltar by our everyday standards and still be capable of oozing like a very thick liquid under the tremendous forces at work far below the earth's surface. Apparently Wegener had been on the right track after all.

Wegener died while on another expedition to Greenland in 1930. He set out alone across the ice cap on the morning of November 1 (his birthday) to secure provisions for a manned inland outpost and never returned. His body was discovered several days later. He had died of a heart attack. Wegener was buried on the ice cap and lies there to this day, his grave marked with his skis.

In the decades following his death, other scientists, notably the great Harry Hess of Princeton, refined Wegener's original, slightly flawed model of continental movements. In the process,

Wegener's concept of continental displacement became known as *continental drift* and finally as *plate tectonics,* the basis of all modern geology.

According to the modern theory of plate tectonics, the earth's crust is broken up into roughly a dozen major plates that float on the denser rock below, called the *asthenosphere,* much as icebergs float in water. The plates vary in thickness from about ten to fifty miles and show a wide range of ages. Parts of the North American crustal plate, for example, are among the oldest exposed rocks on earth at 2.5 billion years or more, while the neighboring Pacific plate is relatively young.

Crustal plates are formed along *midocean ridges,* a system of cracks in the earth's crust where molten rock from the interior rises to the surface, cools, and solidifies. (Not all midocean ridges are found in the middle of oceans; they acquired that name because the first one was discovered in mid-Atlantic by sonar-bearing naval vessels during World War II.) As the rock rises from below and cools, it pushes previously formed crustal rock off to either side of the ridge, in much the same fashion as goods riding a conveyer belt.

This phenomenon is called *sea-floor spreading* and proceeds much faster at some points than others. Off the western coast of South America, sea-floor spreading is taking place at a phenomenal rate of about six inches per year, while in mid-Atlantic the figure is only about an inch per year. So in the lifetime of an average person, New York and Lisbon move about six feet farther apart.

Consequently, crustal plates are constantly in motion. It takes tremendous energy to move a continent even half an inch per year, and scientists are still unsure where all that energy comes from. Rejecting Wegener's concept of flight from the poles, geologist Arthur Holmes of the University of Edinburgh suggested the continents were impelled by giant *convection cells,* churning vortices of hot rock in the earth's mantle. The convection cells were thought to move the continents along in somewhat the same manner as gears driving the treads of a tank. this mechanism seemed much more plausible than Wegener's *Polflucht.*

Yet now this picture, too, has been altered by fresh research. Recent estimates have shown that convection cells could supply only about a tenth of the energy needed to move a crustal plate the size of, say, North America. Moreover, computer-assisted tomography (CAT) analysis of earthquake data—a technology originally developed for medicine and later applied to geology—have given us a detailed look into the mantle and revealed that there is much more inside than a set of convection cells.

In CAT analysis, data from earthquake-recording instruments is fed into a computer and used to produce a three-dimensional image of density gradients in the mantle by comparing the speeds of earthquake waves passing through the rock. The waves move faster through relatively dense, cool rock and more slowly through hotter, relatively "thin" zones. The resulting picture looks as odd to us as Mallet's earthquake map did to his contemporaries.

Inside the mantle, giant streams of rock appear to be rising and descending in a pattern reminiscent of a Henry Moore sculpture. One great "plume" of hot rock, for example, is rising beneath British Columbia and the Pacific Northwest of the United States. This phenomenon accounts for the towering volcanic mountains to be found in that corner of North America, including the recently active Mount St. Helens. The dynamics of the mantle, as revealed by computer analysis of earthquake data, are proving to be much more complex than anyone previously suspected.

Even more intriguing is recent evidence from a computer analysis of the fit among the various crustal plates. Though most modern geologists presume the earth has always been about the size it is now (roughly eight thousand miles in diameter), a computerized projection of crustal plate movements back to the time of Pangaea—roughly 180 million years ago, about when the age of dinosaurs was getting under way—suggests that our world was then much smaller than today. The plate boundaries match up only moderately well if one assumes the earth 180 million years ago was identical in size to the globe today. But if one assumes the earth in the dinosaurs' day had only about four-fifths its present volume, the fit is much better.

Do we actually live on a swelling world? The evidence is inconclusive but has tantalized geologists for more than half a century. In 1933 a geologist named Otto Hilgenberg was among the first to propose that the modern earth has a much greater diameter than it had in the distant past. Hilgenberg suggested that the continental crust of the earth, some seven hundred million years ago, formed a complete, unbroken shell covering the total surface of a globe only about 60 percent as wide as the world we live on today.

Hilgenberg's thoughts on the earth's diameter were largely ignored for the next two decades, then were resurrected at a symposium convened by Professor Warren Carey at the University of Tasmania in Hobart in the 1950s. Carey himself brought up the subject of Hilgenberg's work, and it probably sounded preposterous at the time, for Wegener's hypothesis of moving continents was still dismissed by many geologists as quackery. Hilgenberg's vision of an inflating earth, then, must have seemed even more farfetched.

There was no way of testing Hilgenberg's hypothesis because no one had yet fixed any ages for the thin oceanic crust underlying the seas. But if the crust beneath the seas was sufficiently younger than the rock of the continents, then Hilgenberg's hypothesis might stand a chance.

Slowly, from oceanographic expeditions and commercial drilling operations at sea, the data came in. And they seemed to support Hilgenberg's suggestion. The oceanic crust, generally speaking, was younger than continental crust. But the strongest evidence in favor of Hilgenberg came from a study of "passive" continental margins—those that are not being twisted and distorted by collisions between plates.

The shores of the Atlantic Ocean are good examples of passive margins. Overall they have remained much the same as when Pangaea split apart and sent the Americas drifting westward, about 180 million years ago, opening up the Atlantic Ocean basin in the process. The coasts have not been warped dramatically, as the shores of the Pacific have been by collision between the Pacific plate and the continental plates around it. So we should be able to fit the pieces of this vast Atlantic jigsaw back together, with the aid of computers, to see if they match up adequately on a globe with the current diameter of ours.

They don't—not quite. Look at South America and Africa. Try fitting the east coast of South America alongside the west coast of Africa, and the fit is only fairly good. The big "hump" of the Brazilian shore roughly matches the indentation on western Africa, but on a finer level of detail the fit is poor. The farther north and south one goes, the more space shows between the shores of the two continents. Big gaps appear between South America and Africa about where Argentina and the mouth of the Amazon stand today. Geologists call these gaps *gores*, and they really should not be there today if the earth's diameter was the same 180 million years ago as it is now.

Can we make the gores disappear by choosing a smaller diameter for the ancient earth? Let us assume the earth then was in fact smaller than today. If we pick a diameter for the globe of about 80 percent of the present figure, and reconstruct the fit of South America and Africa, the correspondence this time is excellent! Not only do the big bumps and indentations match up, but the little features on them do as well. The gores disappear, and the resulting picture is thoroughly satisfying to a geographer's mind.

But what if nature has added a few pieces to the puzzle since Pangaea broke apart? Suppose the gores represent new crust produced since the breakup of Pangaea. Could oceanic crust have materialized from somewhere in amounts sufficient to fill the gores?

There is no evidence for it. A highly selective and localized process of caulking would have had to occur to cover the gores, and as far as we know, the earth does not form crust in that pattern. We are left, then, with the probable conclusion that the earth some 180 million years ago was only about four-fifths its present diameter and had roughly half its current volume and two-thirds its modern surface area.

So something appears to have been increasing the area of the globe. The earth does seem to be swelling, just as Hilgenberg suggested half a century ago.

This comes as a shocker for geologists who traditionally have believed in an earth of constant diameter, just as scientists several generations before clung to the tenets of diluvianism. In a 1984 article for the journal *New Scientist*, Dr. Hugh Owen of the British Museum wrote:

> The geological and geophysical implications of such earth expansion are so profound that most geologists and geophysicists shy away from them. . . .
>
> I cannot offer any firm physical explanation of why the earth is expanding. But geophysicists often conveniently forget that [neither] can they offer a firm physical theory to explain continental displacement.

What might be responsible for "fattening" our world? No one knows. Is this where some of that extra "push" needed to move the continents came from? Possibly. A simple experiment will show why.

Inflate a toy balloon partway and hold it closed. Now draw rough outlines of the continents on its surface. Inflate the balloon farther, and the outlines will move apart from one another because the balloon is swelling. If Hilgenberg was correct, this mechanism—operating on a global scale—could have provided the mechanical energy for the redistribution of continents.

As the swelling-earth hypothesis shows, it will be a long time before we understand fully how the earth's active interior affects the crustal plates on its surface. Owen points out that "the acceptance of continental displacement as real initiated a revolution in the earth sciences. The evidence for earth expansion suggests that the revolution is far from over."

Another revolutionary idea, with implications for the study of earthquakes, is the "deep gas" hypothesis put forward some years ago by Dr. Thomas Gold of Cornell University. An astronomer who founded and directed for twenty years Cornell University's Center for Radiophysics and Space Research, Gold is perhaps best known as the coauthor, with astronomers Herman Bondi and Fred Hoyle, of the once controversial "steady state" model of the universe. The steady state model was based on the assumption that the universe did not originate in a cataclysmic initial "big bang," as is believed today, but rather the universe is in a steady state of expansion, with new matter coming into existence spontaneously all the time as the galaxies move apart. Though now largely discredited, the steady state theory played an important part in the genesis of modern thinking about cosmology.

Just as the steady state theory began with a bold and unconventional assumption about the universe, Gold's deep gas hypothesis is founded on an idea that runs counter to the traditional wisdom of geology. Hydrocarbons (in a general sense, petroleum compounds) buried in the earth are commonly thought to be derived from the long-buried remains of plants and animals. Their remains, buried under sediment in ocean basins, are widely believed to have been converted into hydrocarbons by pressure and heat deep underground, as the sediments in which the organisms lay buried were turned to

rock. When oil companies tap underground reserves of petroleum (says the conventional theory), they are robbing the
graves, so to speak, of prehistoric fauna.

Hydrocarbons are organic chemicals. That means they are
based on the carbon atom, the element that makes life as we
know it possible. A typical hydrocarbon consists of a long string
of carbon atoms linked together and flanked by rows of
hydrogen atoms—hence the name "hydrocarbons." The carbon-based character of hydrocarbons makes it reasonable to
assume, then, that they had their origin in living things, ages
ago.

Or is that assumption reasonable? Gold knew that organic
material had been found in meteorites. These meteorites are
called *carbonaceous chondrites* because they contain carbon-based
material. Some of the compounds found in these meteorites
would be considered of biological origin if found on earth. But
the meteorites are clearly not from our world. They originated
instead in distant corners of our solar system, if not in other
systems entirely. In fact, some of our neighbor planets, such as
Jupiter and Saturn, are so rich in hydrocarbons that visionary
scientists in the 1960s briefly considered "mining" them with
special spacecraft to supply fuel for an energy-starved Earth of
the future.

The chondrites set Gold to thinking. He imagined that the
small pieces of solid material that coalesced to form our world,
billions of years ago, carried hydrocarbons with them. The hydrocarbons were buried deep inside the earth as the planet
took shape and (Gold imagined) might be seeping back to the
surface. Perhaps "roaring" is a better word: if hydrocarbon-
bearing material has been "cooking" inside our world for billions of years, and releasing hydrocarbon gases all that time,
the gases must build up terrific pressure. That pressure might
itself set off earthquakes. At the very least it would cause great
outbursts of gas through cracks in the earth's crust whenever
an earthquake or other disturbance created a pathway to the
surface through which the gas might escape.

A full discussion of Gold's idea is beyond the scope of this
book. But the deep gas hypothesis, if correct, would explain
some puzzling features of earthquakes. One is the phenomenon called *earthquake light*. This is a pale glow that has been
frequently seen, and reportedly photographed on one or two

occasions, in the night sky near the horizon just prior to and during major quakes. Earthquake light has been observed so often that its existence is hard to deny, but geologists have had trouble explaining it. One Soviet geologist in the 1960s suggested that the light might be the glow produced by atmospheric molecules stimulated by electrons—negatively charged subatomic particles—released from the earth by a quake. The electrons, in theory, would "kick" the air molecules into a higher state of energy and force them to give out photons, or particles of light, in the same way a neon sign glows when plugged in.

This explanation was shaky, however, as were most others until the deep gas hypothesis came along. If some earthquakes really are accompanied by outbursts of primordial methane from the earth's interior, then the mystery of earthquake light becomes easy to understand. The flammable hydrocarbon mixes with oxygen in the atmosphere, is ignited by static electricity or other ignition sources at the ground, and burns with an eerie pale light like that from a gas range in a darkened room.

Escaping methane from underground might also be responsible for another odd phenomenon associated with many quakes along seashores. There are hundreds of incidents where eyewitnesses to an earthquake by the sea noted the waters bubbling like tap water in a teakettle, even though there was no heat source at hand to set the waters boiling. A mysterious bubbling was observed off the southern California coast at the time of the 1971 San Fernando earthquake, for example. Might the bubbles have been methane rising to the surface? Possibly. We will explore that thought in more detail later in this book, in connection with past and future quakes along the borders between crustal plates—particularly in California.

The plates, growing steadily at midocean ridges, cannot keep growing forever. Eventually they bump against other crustal plates. When that happens, dramatic things occur.

The plates may hit head-on and push up great mountain ranges. These are known to geologists as *compressional features* because the mountains arise where blocks of crust are compressed together. The opposite of compressional features are *tensional features.* These often take the form of valleys created where blocks of crust are pulling away from one another.

Alternatively, one plate may ride up over the other, and the loser in this conflict will be pushed down, or *subducted*, into the mantle. As the descending crustal plate melts in the hot mantle, its lighter components float back upward, like hot-air balloons rising in the atmosphere. This rising material occasionally finds its way to the surface through fissures in the crustal rock. When molten rock spurts out of the ground, we call it a *volcano;* and that is why volcanic mountains are frequently found where crustal plates collide. Mount St. Helens, for example, is the product of the ongoing collision between the North American crustal plate and the smaller Juan de Fuca plate, off the coasts of Oregon and the state of Washington.

Collisions like these are not gentle meetings. Billions of tons of rock, smashed together by terrific forces, produce another kind of natural violence—earthquakes.

A modern chart of crustal plate boundaries shows that they match up almost precisely with the earthquake map that Mallet drew more than a century ago. The high-intensity earthquake zone in the Mediterranean marks where the African crustal plate is being pushed northward into Europe. The collision between the Indian subcontinent and Asia has generated a hotbed of seismic activity along the Himalayas and the mountains of Afghanistan and Iran. Where the Pacific crustal plate meets Asia, in an arc stretching from Siberia south to the tropical waters off Mindanao, earthquakes and volcanoes are commonplace. And across the Pacific, where the oceanic crustal plate grinds against western North America, lies the most quake-prone state in our nation: California.

Most of California is very young by geological standards. California as we see it today was formed only within the last few million years. That is almost yesterday on the 4.5-billion-year time scale of the earth. The land that is modern California started forming about thirty million years ago, as the North American plate inched westward and collided with a midocean ridge running north and south through the Pacific Ocean.

Something had to give, and something did. The relatively thick continental plate rode up and over the oceanic plate and the midocean ridge, burying them under miles of rock. But though the ridge was annihilated, the fires under it were not extinguished. Molten rock continued to seep upward where the ridge had stood, generating volcanic activity under the western coast of the continent. This is why so much of California's terrain consists of *igneous rock,* meaning it solidified directly from a molten state. The California landscape was generated in large part by that buried midocean ridge. (California still has active volcanoes. Mount Lassen, in northern California, erupted during World War I with such violence that it destroyed hundreds of square miles of surrounding forest in a single outburst of ash and superheated gas.)

Vulcanism, however, was not the only process at work shaping California. The collision between the two crustal plates heaved up towering mountains and crumpled the crustal rocks into fantastically convoluted patterns. This is why California has the most complex geology of any state in the nation. Its crust has been mangled by the continent's advance for more than fifty million years, all the while erosion and volcanic eruptions were complicating the picture still further. Trying to comprehend California's geology is like trying to undo the Gordian knot without the aid of Alexander's sword.

Look at a geological map of California, and you will see a network of dark lines like the wrinkles in an elephant's hide. These lines are *faults,* or cracks in the earth's crust. They mark areas where chunks of crust are moving, or have moved, relative to one another.

If the crust on both sides of a fault line is immobile, geologists say that fault is *dormant,* or incapable of producing earthquakes. Motion along a fault line means the fault is active—a quake source. California abounds in active faults, crisscrossed and interconnected in a pattern as complex as the human skeleton; and the backbone of the skeleton, so to speak, is the world's most famous fault line, the great San Andreas Fault, which caused the 1906 San Francisco disaster. The crust on either side of the fault shifted position about twenty feet horizontally that day. There was little or no vertical motion, because the San Andreas is what geologists call a *strike-slip fault,* along which up-and-down movements are negligible.

The San Andreas Fault extends along the coast of California for more than five hundred miles, from San Diego in the south to a point on the fog-wrapped shores near San Francisco. At some points it appears as a dramatic break in the crust, like Elkhorn Scarp, but more often the fault is barely perceptible to observers on the ground. The only clearly visible signs of its

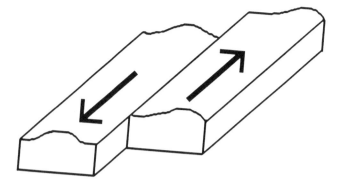

Fault Lines: A *fault* is a crack, or "discontinuity," in the earth's crust along which blocks of crust move relative to each other. Shown here is a strike-slip fault, where displacement is horizontal. California's San Andreas Fault is an example of a strike-slip fault. *(Courtesy of Allan Frank)*

presence near San Francisco are Lake San Andreas, a long and narrow lake that lies parallel to the fault just south of the city, and Mussel Rock, a slight offset in the shore where the fault runs out to sea at Daly City, a southern suburb. Development has eliminated many traces of the fault on the surface; the blades of bulldozers have so reworked the land that only by looking at a geological map or an aerial photo can one tell where the San Andreas Fault runs. Some of its smaller, tributary faults are easier to spot than the San Andreas Fault itself; the Hayward fault on the east shore of San Francisco Bay, for example, shows as the dividing line between the hills and the plain on which the east bay cities are built.

Generally speaking, the San Andreas Fault marks the boundary between the Pacific crustal plate and the North American plate. The former is sliding northward relative to the latter, but not very smoothly. Instead of slipping past each other at a steady rate, the two crustal plates tend to "stick together" and build up tension, which gets released every century or so in the form of a major earthquake. The plates move very slowly by our everyday standards; North America and the Pacific plate shift their relative positions only about an inch and a half per year, on the average. But over a century or so, the displacement builds up to the point where only a big quake can relieve the resulting strain.

The San Andreas Fault is actually not a single fault at all, but rather two different fault systems that formed at different times, in different ways. Northern California's half of the San Andreas Fault is older and less active than the southern half. The northern San Andreas shows a relative displacement of only about half an inch per year, while slippage along the southern part is about four times greater, or roughly two inches annually.

How these two branches of the San Andreas Fault formed is an interesting story that explains some peculiar features of the geology of California and western Mexico. To illustrate, imagine you could look down on California and Mexico from outer space some twenty-five million years ago. The landscape below would look vaguely familiar. You would see the familiar snow-capped bulk of the Sierra Nevada range at about its present location. You would not see the unmistakable outline of San Francisco Bay, however, because that corner of California had not yet formed. Likewise, the land to the south of the Sierra Nevada would look unfamiliar. The Salton Sea basin was as yet unformed, and Baja California—the long, narrow strip of land separated from the Mexican mainland by the Gulf of California —did not exist twenty-five million years ago. It was still attached to the mainland.

But things began to happen fast along the California coast as North America moved relentlessly westward. A sliver of crust several hundred miles long began slipping north along the western edge of the continent, nudged along by the relative northward motion of the Pacific plate. This chunk of crust spent the next five or six million years moving some two hundred miles to where northern California is now. Where it touched the North American mainland, the dividing line between the continent and the northward-moving sliver of crust from the south became the northern portion of the San Andreas Fault. (Though some popular accounts of the fault's formation make it sound as if a razor-edged cut along the San Andreas divides the Pacific plate from the North American plate, the division between the two plates is actually much less clear. For example, the tiny Farallon Islands, about forty miles west of the Golden Gate, lie in the Pacific Ocean yet are made of rock "splinters" shaved off the North American plate to the east.)

Later, this same combination of processes—fragmentation

and northward migration—repeated itself. Another sliver of crust broke off from the Mexican mainland and began edging northward. As it did so, it swung away from the mainland of Mexico and opened up the Gulf of California. But this time the forces acting on the northward-moving block of crust were different. There was an obstacle in the way: the Sierra Nevada, a towering mountain range with peaks almost two miles high.

Rooted deep in the mantle, the huge granitic mass of the Sierra Nevada blocked the northward motion of the crustal segment from Mexico. Unable to slip around the corner, so to speak, the ribbon of crust ground and shoved against the Sierra Nevada and pushed up another, smaller set of mountains, known today the Transverse Ranges because they run crosswise to the Sierra Nevada. The Transverse Ranges mark the point where Baja California got hung up on the older mountain range.

All this happened about five million years ago, almost yesterday on the scale of geologic time. Since then, bits and pieces of Baja California's block of crust have been making their way slowly around the southern tip of the Sierra Nevada, like shavings from a nutmeg being ground. Santa Barbara is situated on one of those crustal fragments. Los Angeles is located on another such shard of crust, one that has not quite made its way around the Sierra Nevada.

Where these former parts of the Mexican mainland join up with North America, we find a complex pattern made up of the southern San Andreas Fault and its tributaries, such as the Garlock Fault, which branches off from the San Andreas a few miles east of Santa Barbara and runs inland through the Mojave Desert. Near the Garlock Fault lies the White Wolf Fault, of which we will see more later.

Two other fault lines, the Elsinore Fault and the San Jacinto Fault, run parallel to the coast just southeast of Los Angeles, between San Diego and the San Bernardino Mountains. Branching off from the San Andreas and then rejoining it later, like a highway detour, is the San Gabriel Fault, which at its closest approach comes within forty miles of the Los Angeles city limits. And to the west, greater Los Angeles is bounded by the highly active Newport-Inglewood Fault, which follows the coast south past San Diego and across the border into Mexico.

All these faults are active; all are potential killers. So Los Angeles is virtually surrounded with earthquake sources.

Where the Garlock and San Andreas faults meet, one finds the epicenter of the great 1857 Fort Tejon earthquake. The 1952 Kern County earthquake was also centered on the Garlock Fault, about thirty miles to the northeast of the Fort Tejon event. These two quakes occurred within a feature called the *Palmdale bulge,* a vast uplift of rock about the size of Connecticut, created where the Garlock and San Andreas faults come together near the city of Palmdale, about forty miles north of Los Angeles on the edge of the Mojave Desert.

The Palmdale bulge began to edge upward in the spring of 1958. It rose slowly, only a little over half an inch per year; but even such a tiny uplift involved billions of tons of rock, which in turn involved a serious quake potential. Over the next fifteen years, the bulge rose roughly ten inches. One report said, in a masterpiece of understatement, that the bulge's elevation represented "considerable subsurface strain." In California, "subsurface strain" translates as earthquake risk.

The Palmdale bulge has caused Californians serious concern over the past few decades, because no one enjoyed thinking about what might happen if the bulge came crashing down all at once. But the bulge has been shrinking lately, and the mention of it no longer makes Angelenos anxious.

That is not to say, however, that greater Los Angeles is in any less danger from earthquakes. The Palmdale bulge, as we have seen, is not the sole quake source in southern California. Numerous other known faults are capable of setting off major quakes in Los Angeles and its vicinity. And there are probably other, equally dangerous local faults of which scientists know nothing because they lie buried under soil and sediment. Let us look next at just how those faults can spread destruction and why some areas of greater Los Angeles are at especially great risk from the next superquake.

3

Other Quake Dangers

One striking aspect of earth-quakes is how selectively they destroy things. One house may be demolished completely in an earthquake, while another similar home nearby suffers only modest damage. Why?

The answer, in many cases, is a process called *liquefaction*. It is just what its name indicates: the transformation of relatively firm ground into something that behaves like a liquid.

Liquefaction can destroy whole communities by annulling the firmness of the earth on which they rest. Since liquefaction plays an important part in our story, let us look at the phenomenon and how it causes damage.

Liquefaction is defined formally as "the transformation of a granular material from a solid state into a liquefied state as a consequence of increased pore-water pressures." That definition may need a little translation.

Granular material, for our purposes, means unconsolidated ground, namely soil, sand, or other sedimentary stuff that has not been turned into rock. If you live along a coastline or near a river that has a floodplain, chances are your home is built on top of unconsolidated granular material. And even if you live inland, you may still sit atop such material. Some major cities in America's heartland are built on unconsolidated sediments that once were mud and sand at the bottom of lakes or inland seas.

But simply being unconsolidated does not make the ground under you prone to liquefaction. Some other factors are at work, such as *pore-water pressure.*

Wherever there is liquid water in the soil, the water fills tiny spaces, or pores, in between soil grains. This water exerts pressure on the grains. Ordinarily they rest on top of one another like goods on a store shelf, making it possible for the soil to bear the weight of homes, office buildings, and highways. The water in the pores does not exert enough pressure on the grains to push them out of place. If the pressure rose sharply, the soil would lose strength and be unable to hold up buildings.

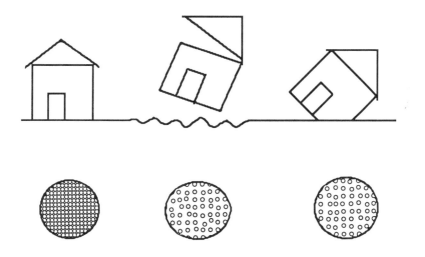

Liquefaction: This highly stylized diagram shows how S-waves cause liquefaction and damage to buildings. At left in the diagram, soil particles (inside circle) are resting undisturbed. In center, S-waves have increased pore-water pressure in the soil and made the soil behave temporarily as a liquid, with drastic effects on the building above. At right the soil slowly returns to its normal state. *(Courtesy of Allan Frank)*

Unfortunately, that is just what happens in many earthquakes. When the shock from a quake travels through the wet unconsolidated soil, it increases water pressure in the pores. You can see how this happens by performing a simple demonstration in the kitchen. Fill a plastic sandwich bag with water and close it. Place the bag in the sink and hit the bag firmly with your fist. The impact of your hand raises water pressure inside the bag, and it will burst. Here your fist is equivalent to the vibrations from an earthquake, and the water pressure inside the bag stands for the pore-water pressure in a quake-shaken soil. And just as the change in pressure creates a watery mess in your sink, it creates a similar situation in liquefying soil.

The increased pressure jiggles the soil grains out of place. They are no longer stacked neatly on top of one another. Instead they swirl around chaotically in response to the quake and the change it has caused in pore-water pressure. The result is that the soil turns into a kind of soup.

What happens to buildings above when a soil liquefies? About what would happen if the structures were built on corn-meal mush. They slide, sink, topple, roll over, or collapse entirely, because their underpinnings have started to behave as a liquid. A house may sink like a torpedoed ship when the soil beneath it liquefies. At the same time, any underground structure that is buoyant—say, an empty fuel tank—may bob upward through the liquefied soil like a submarine rising to the surface. Soil liquefaction is one reason that anyone seriously concerned about surviving an earthquake should heed the biblical warning against building one's house on sand.

But liquefaction's effects are not confined to creating soupy soil. Liquefied soil is also much more liable to oscillate, or vibrate strongly, than other materials are. So a liquefied soil can amplify the S-waves from a quake and increase their destructive power manifold.

This is why, in the San Francisco earthquake of 1906, quake damage (as opposed to the fire damage that followed) was worst in the parts of town that were built on landfill. The fill was unconsolidated and moist. As the S-waves surged through town, the soil under these neighborhoods liquefied and the waves were amplified by the fluid sediment through which they passed. In other words, the ripples from the quake were bigger in the liquefied fill than they were in other neighborhoods where the underlying material was firmer. Bigger waves meant more destruction.

If the effect of liquefaction on earthquake waves is unclear to you, try another simple demonstration. Drop a book on the floor and it will not generate much of a vibration. That is because the floor is made of wood, concrete, or some other consolidated material. The book's fall will generate a little shear wave, but one barely strong enough to feel, much less see.

Now drop that same book on a waterbed. This time the wave is easy to see, because the water inside the mattress is a thoroughly unconsolidated material. In the San Francisco quake, portions of the earth under the city were liquefied until they had almost the same properties as water. So the earthquake vibrations had their greatest effect there.

The effects of liquefaction, incidentally, are not confined to structural damage. Look back at chapter 1 and reread Mark Twain's description of the earthquake he experienced in San Francisco. He mentions that many people suffered motion sickness during and after the quake. That is because liquefaction of the soil created, on land, the same rolling and pitching motions that cause seasickness on the ocean. About the only difference was that the waves were moving through liquefied soil instead of seawater.

Liquefaction poses still another peril. Suppose soil at the surface is comparatively dry and hangs together, but soil a few yards down has more water in it and liquefies. What happens then?

The result can be calamitous if the soil is on a slope. The coherent soil at the surface remains bound together in a giant slab—but the liquefied soil below does not. Instead the liquefied soil acts as a lubricant, like a layer of oil, and allows the slab above to slide downslope. The slope need not be steep for this to happen. An incline of two or three degrees is sufficient in some cases. An event like this can carry away a whole neighborhood.

How susceptible is the L.A. region to liquefaction in the next superquake? Some parts of the metropolitan area are reasonably safe from liquefaction damage; others face a serious risk that the soil under them will liquefy and cause destruction. It is seldom possible to tell, just by looking at soil, how prone it is to liquefaction, because many different factors contribute to liquefaction potential.

The age and type of soil are important. Generally speaking, moist, recently deposited, sandy or silty soils where groundwater comes close to the surface are the most dangerous where liquefaction is concerned. Examples would be beach sand or floodplain sediments along a river.

Particle size also counts for a lot. The more gravel and boulders you have in soil, the less likely it is to liquefy during a quake. A soil made up of 85 percent gravelly sand, with only 15 percent finer material, is less likely to liquefy. The safest kind of soil in this regard would be a coarse mixture of gravel and boulders, with 15–20 percent fine material. Chunks of rock in such soils are so big and heavy that a rise in pore-water pressure during an earthquake is not likely to move them very much. To use a naval analogy, gravels and boulders are somewhat like cruisers and battleships, which can ride out a big wave more easily than a tiny rowboat can.

One recent U.S. Geological Survey publication rates parts of greater Los Angeles for their liquefaction potential. Here is a summary of how the report rates several areas:

- *San Fernando Valley.* Despite the shaking it took in the 1971 earthquake, the San Fernando Valley is in good shape, generally speaking, where liquefaction is involved. Most areas show only a medium to low susceptibility, and some spots, such as the Verdugo Mountains near Burbank, are rated very low. The trouble starts where groundwater comes close to the surface, as it does in a strip of soil stretching approximately from North Hollywood to Canoga Park. Portions of that area—though not all—show a high to very high liquefaction potential.
- *San Gabriel Valley.* Areas of high liquefaction potential are found near Azusa, Walnut, and a point about three miles south of Monterey Park. Fortunately, most of the San Gabriel Valley rates low to very low.
- *Los Angeles basin.* Here the risk of liquefaction is generally higher than in the previous two areas, partly because much of the city is built on unconsolidated stuff and partly because areas near the Pacific Ocean have groundwater levels

that come very close to the surface, making liquefaction there more likely.

Long Beach will be in great peril from liquefaction whenever the next superquake hits Los Angeles. The U.S. Geological Survey's map of liquefaction potential in the Los Angeles basin rates Long Beach medium to high on its scale. Terminal Island is in this danger zone. So is Seal Beach, a few miles down the coast. The Bell neighborhood, between Downey and Maywood, is another high-risk area. Others may be found near Lakewood Village and Artesia.

The most dangerous places of all, the publication judges, lie on the shore between Santa Monica and the Palos Verdes Hills. This strip of coast—about eighteen miles long—includes Manhattan Beach, Hermosa Beach, and Redondo Beach. These communities have a very high potential for liquefaction because they rest atop recently deposited stream channel and levee deposits where groundwater rises to less than ten feet from the surface.

• *Orange County.* Large areas of Orange County run a high risk of liquefaction in the next major earthquake. The area around Los Alamitos rates high on the scale of liquefaction potential. Indeed, almost the whole area within the boundaries of Highway 101 (about ten to fifteen miles from the Pacific), the San Joaquin Hills to the southeast, and the Los Angeles county line to the northwest falls within the medium to very high range.

In some places a distance of only a few yards separates a high-risk area from a safe haven. In Corona del Mar, for example, the oceanfront runs a very high risk of liquefaction, while the San Joaquin Hills, practically within shouting distance of the water, are ranked very low on the liquefaction scale. The same situation exists at Huntington Beach and at Costa Mesa. Santa Ana is a low-risk spot on the U.S. Geological Survey map, surrounded by a "moat" of medium to very high liquefaction potential. Another "island" of relative safety exists near Anaheim, around the intersection of Routes 101 and 18.

• *Upper Santa Ana River basin.* The San Andreas Fault runs along the edge of this part of the L.A. area, so liquefaction should be a cause for concern here. Unfortunately, estimates of liquefaction potential made even a few years ago may not be valid now, because groundwater in this area has been rising rapidly, in some places so fast that it has flooded cellars. The publication, however, lists several areas where liquefaction is likely to occur if "cohesionless granular sediment" (as the U.S. Geological Survey puts it) is present:

1. The Santa Ana River channel and portions of its adjacent floodplains, between the Jacinto Fault and the Prado Dam.

2. The area around San Bernardino, especially northeast of the San Jacinto Fault.

3. Several small areas where groundwater may build up on a seasonal basis. These spots are located near La Verne, Pomona, and Claremont; the Upland area; and the San Antonio area.

4. Areas of shallow groundwater in the vicinity of Mentone, Lytle Creek Canyon, Yucaipa, San Timeon Canyon, and Mill Creek.

Among the comparatively safe areas in the upper Santa Ana River basin are Ontario, Mira Loma, Edgemont, and Chino (low to very low potential).

If sediments on land can hold enough water to pose a serious liquefaction risk, what about sediments offshore? What happens if a major earthquake sets off undersea landslides or other disturbances and transfers some of its energy to the waters? Here we return to the scary topic of tsunamis, or seismic sea waves, and the threat they may pose to southern California shores in the next superquake.

Whenever a major earthquake occurs on or near a shoreline, emergency preparedness officials start to worry about tsunamis. Though familiar phenomena in the world's oceans, and especially in the Pacific, tsunamis are still poorly understood. Tsunamis have a variety of causes, from earthquakes and volcanic eruptions to typhoons; but it is uncertain where all the energy in certain tsunamis comes from. Some tsunamis seem too large and powerful for the events that generated them, while some truly catastrophic events, which would seem to have the potential for producing towering tsunamis capable of wiping out shorelines five thousand miles away, may give rise to no more than a ripple.

Tsunamis have left their mark on literature, religion, and

art. The biblical stories of Noah's Flood and Moses' parting of the Red Sea are widely believed to be mythologized accounts of tsunamis, as is the Atlantis legend. Some well-known Norse legends bear a striking similarity to the projected effects of tsunamis hitting the coast of Scandinavia, and certain Native American tribes have legends of the final day of the world, when mountain-high waves would submerge the land and obliterate all the evil works of humankind. Hiroshige's famous print *The Great Wave*, perhaps the best-known graphic in Japanese history, is a beautiful depiction of a giant, curling wave approaching from the sea off Japan's coastline, with the graceful white cone of Mount Fuji rising in the distance. So skillful and attractive is the composition that one almost overlooks the boats about to be engulfed and smashed by the wave.

Tsunamis are the subject of numerous misconceptions. The popular image of tsunamis is that of a single great wave that rises from the sea, engulfs whatever lies in its path onshore, then returns to the ocean, leaving total destruction in its wake. This picture is inaccurate. The reality is even less pleasant. Tsunamis tend to occur in trains of perhaps six or seven waves rather than individually, so that the unfortunate coastline is hit not merely once, but again and again as the wave train comes crashing ashore.

When a tsunami reaches land, it does not always take the form of a huge, crashing breaker. It may manifest itself instead as a sudden upward surge of the sea, like a ripple moving down a shaken carpet. Bottom configuration near the land does much to determine how a tsunami affects the shore. A gentle offshore slope may slow down the wave and weaken it considerably before it arrives, while steeper slopes may permit the wave to hit with much of its initial punch intact. Reefs and other such offshore obstacles do little to halt large tsunamis; the waves simply ride over them undeterred.

Sometimes a tsunami will seem to gain strength mysteriously or weaken and die without explanation. Complex and enigmatic forces are at work in tsunamis, and it will be a long time before we understand those forces thoroughly.

Huge and destructive though it may be, a tsunami is really little more than a moving shock front of energy passing from one water molecule to another in much the same fashion as an

S-wave from an earthquake on land. The water molecules themselves are not swept along with the tsunami. They oscillate slightly as the wave passes, but afterward they resume their original positions.

Only when the tsunami nears shore does it start to become a physical object. As the water beneath becomes more and more shallow, the wave is pushed upward and rises to form a familiar wave pattern. Under some circumstances, a breaking tsunami may send water rushing more than a mile overland. Ranges of ten miles or more are not unheard of, where rivers and estuaries give the wave an easy route inland.

The Japanese are in particular danger from seismic sea waves, because their land is so quake-prone and because it has such a long and densely populated coastline. The tsunami that came ashore at Sanriku on June 15, 1896, is said to have been one hundred feet high. That wave completely obliterated communities along the water. Casualties were estimated later at more than twenty-five thousand.

The Hawaiian Islands are also subject to destructive tsunamis on occasion. The most famous Hawaiian tsunami struck the island shortly after midnight on April 1, 1946. More than 175 persons were killed in Hilo, and damage was estimated at $25 million (or perhaps $150 million in today's currency).

Observers of that tsunami who had the good fortune to be on high ground when the wave arrived put its height at about sixteen feet. Here is part of one eyewitness account of the wave:

> At first there was . . . a dull rumble like a distant train. . . . As our eyes searched for the source of the ominous noise, a pale wall of tumbling water, the broken crest of the . . . wave, was caught in the dim light thrown across the water by the lights of Hilo. . . . Turning around, we saw a flood of water pouring up the estuary. The top of the inrushing current caught in the steel-girder roadway at the south half of the bridge and sent a spray of water high into the air. Seconds later, brilliant blue-white electrical flashes . . . signaled that the wave had crossed the seawall and buffer zone and was washing into the town with crushing force. . . .

The wave's progress was marked with bright electrical flashes as it caused short circuits while running through the city. The observers just quoted heard "dull, grating sounds" from buildings being ground together and sharp cracking noises as telephone poles were snapped in two by the wave. About one minute after passing the bridge, the wave reached a power plant at the southern end of the bay. A dazzling green flash lit up the sky as the power plant failed. Then darkness engulfed Hilo and most of the rest of the island.

Shortly after 2:00 A.M. the waves appeared to have subsided, and a few onlookers decided it was safe to venture into town and take an inventory of damage. They found the streets covered with "thick slimy mud," and fish carried ashore by the wave lay everywhere. The air stank of sewage which had been picked up from its normal dumping point near the mouth of the harbor and washed back into the city. Stores in the business district had been emptied by the wave, which smashed their windows and scattered merchandise around the streets. The streets were also littered with great boulders and smashed automobiles. In some places debris was piled to the second-story level.

After that nightmarish experience, the city of Hilo banned any new construction in the area destroyed by the tsunami. Instead the demolished area was converted into a park, which both improved Hilo's appearance and provided a zone of safety in case another tsunami should come ashore.

Hilo Harbor is especially vulnerable to damage from tsunamis because it is V-shaped, with the downtown area at the apex of the V. This configuration makes the harbor a great natural funnel that concentrates the destructive force of a tsunami on the heart of the city.

The "big island" of Hawaii is also vulnerable to tsunami damage. A party of sleeping campers on the beach at Halape was awakened early on the morning of November 29, 1975, by a moderate earthquake, about 6.2 on the Richter scale. Some of the campers moved away from the water, but the remainder stayed on the beach. About an hour later a 7.2 earthquake occurred. This time the ground motion was so strong that the campers were unable to stand. As they lay helpless on the beach, the waters offshore rose as a tsunami and spilled ashore.

Another, bigger wave followed. The campers on the beach

were swept up and washed into a fissure about twenty feet deep, where the water swirled them around, battering them against rocks and trees that had also been caught in the wave. One camper was killed; another was carried out to sea and never seen again; and more than a dozen others were injured.

A particularly chilling tale of a tsunami's violence was told after a wave slammed into the Chilean coast in 1960. One scientist who studied the tsunami's effects contributed the following account of the disaster to a U.S Navy report published the following year:

> Suddenly, [people on land] noted that the sea was beginning to retreat from the shores, exposing the ocean floor [at] distances well beyond the lowest tides. . . . After fifteen to thirty minutes, the sea returned . . . in a wave that was, in places, over twenty feet high. The wave rushed over the land, covering and carrying away the houses, killing the animals that could not be evacuated and carrying off some of the people who, for one reason or another, had not left their homes. . . .

In one community some five hundred persons were killed because they ignored the warning of the approaching wave or returned to their homes too soon and were caught in the tsunami. In several villages cool-headed *mariscadores*, or shellfish gatherers, walked out on the exposed seabed just before the tsunami's arrival and filled their baskets with bivalves. Then they returned to the safety of high ground moments before the onrushing wall of water reached shore. Four waves struck the coast, the last being the largest. An Aracunian tribe reportedly sacrificed a seven-year-old boy to the sea gods in hopes of calming the waters.

The most famous tsunami in history followed the explosion of the Indonesian volcanic island Krakatoa (also known as Krakatau) in 1883. Located in the Sunda Strait between Java and Sumatra, Krakatoa just over a century ago was a pear-shaped island covered with luxuriant vegetation. Its plant life was destroyed when Krakatoa's fatal eruption began in the spring of 1883. Ash and pumice from the volcano buried the island and the surrounding waters as well; because it is lighter than water, the pumice covered the sea in great floating rafts that sometimes posed a hazard to navigation.

The eruption intensified through early summer, until by late August it was plain that something dreadful was about to happen. Strong earthquakes shook the straits. From the nearby shores, onlookers could see brilliant flashes of light, probably caused by superheated gas escaping from the volcano.

Invisible from the outside, a lethal process was at work inside Krakatoa. Molten rock full of dissolved gases (mostly water vapor) was rising to the surface and encountering seawater, which cooled the rock and, in effect, formed a plug in the throat of the volcano. As the molten rock cooled it lost some of its burden of dissolved gases, which fizzed out a solution in much the same fashion as a freshly opened bottle of champagne. But the gases could not escape because the water at sea level had cut off their escape. So gas pressure built up inside Krakatoa until it reached the bursting point.

Krakatoa blew up on Sunday, August 26, 1883. The explosion was heard three thousand miles away, where the noise was compared to a naval vessel at sea firing its guns. Most of the island of Krakatoa vanished in the explosion. When the smoke cleared, observers could see the blast had sliced the island's southern peak in two vertically, exposing layer upon layer of volcanic rock and ash.

As far as we know, the blast itself killed no one. Most of the estimated thirty thousand to eighty thousand victims of Krakatoa were crushed and drowned in the tsunami following the explosion. Shores within one thousand miles of the volcano were inundated by giant waves that carried away or buried entire towns in a matter of seconds. The tsunami from Krakatoa was visible off the Cape of Good Hope, at the southern tip of Africa, and was detected on tidal gauges in the English Channel. The wave circled the world three times before finally dissipating.

The California coast has been battered by dozens of tsunamis in the past two centuries. Here are a few of them:

- *1812 (date uncertain).* An earthquake near San Francisco produced a tsunami that reportedly caused great damage there. One account, unfortunately not by an eyewitness, says the quake "was so severe as to cause tidal waves that covered the ground where the plaza now is." The earthquake that generated this tsunami is believed to have been centered in the East Bay.

• *December 21, 1812.* This tsunami is better documented than the previous one. It was caused by an earthquake estimated at 7.0–7.5 on the Richter scale, somewhere in or near the Santa Barbara Channel. The waves were large, but their exact height is uncertain. One estimate puts the wave at fifty feet, though its actual height may have been closer to fifteen feet. In any case it was an impressive tsunami and is said to have reached half a mile inland. No deaths were reported.

• *July 24, 1854.* An observer at San Diego reported that the tide rose and fell unexpectedly by about a foot in ten minutes. This observation strongly indicates a tsunami was involved, but no earthquake has been pinpointed as its source.

• *October 26, 1854.* A tsunami was observed at San Francisco following an earthquake there.

• November 1, 1854. Another tsunami was recorded at Angel Island in San Francisco Bay. Though the sea was calm and there was no wind, the island was suddenly battered by high waves for about half an hour.

• *July 10 or 11, 1855.* An earthquake near Los Angeles was accompanied by extremely heavy waves after the last of four shocks. This earthquake is suspected to have occurred onshore, along the Raymond Fault.

• *September 24, 1859.* The source of this tsunami is uncertain, but it had dramatic effects on waters near San Francisco; reports indicate the sea "receded fifteen feet and returned suddenly." The wave ran some fifteen feet up the shores of Half Moon Bay.

• *May 27, 1862.* A strong earthquake at San Diego caused a tsunami in the bay there. There is no mechanical record of the tsunami because the tide gauge was out of order at the time. But one observer recorded his impressions of the wave: "The water in the bay . . . [ran up] on the beach between three and four feet and immediately returned to its usual level." It is not known whether he was referring to horizontal or vertical distance.

• *August 10, 1879.* A sizable tsunami is said to have hit Santa Monica following an earthquake in San Fernando, but no details are available.

• *December 17, 1896.* This tsunami stands as one of the most notable in California history. It rolled into Santa Barbara at 8:00 A.M., "carrying back with it a large section of [a] beautiful and expensive [boulevard]," says one 1898 account of the wave. D. S. McCullough, in a U.S. Geological Survey history of tsunamis along the Pacific Coast, quotes from that same report: "The boulevard was built some five years ago and bulkheaded so securely that it was thought to be impervious to the action of the waves, but the bounding billows carried off a portion of asphaltum and solid masonry, heavy framework, and iron in its receding grasp nearly fifty feet square and eight feet deep. A large sand hill between the boulevard and ordinary high tide was carried completely out to sea."

A local newspaper carried a report of the disaster but described it as an unusually high tide rather than a seismic sea wave: "The flood tide this morning was one of the highest ever known in this city, and the boulevard suffered considerable damage. Between seven and eight o'clock this morning . . . the waves washed over the one-hundred-foot driveway, carrying seaweed to the farthest side and filling the car track with sand. . . . The grassy sand hill between Chapala and State streets on the beach has been washed out, exposing the boulevard front nearly the entire distance."

The paper noted the peculiar conditions that accompanied the wave: "The tide has not been so high for years; even the big washout last spring not being so extensive, the water then coming in under a heavy southeast wind. This time there was no wind for a week." The absence of wind indicates that this so-called flood tide was actually a tsunami.

• *April 18, 1906.* The great San Francisco earthquake appears to have caused a minor tsunami in the bay. Tide gauge records show minor fluctuations in water level at Fort Point, and one observer at Point Arena reported afterward that "at the mouth of the Navarro River, at eight o'clock on the morning of the eighteenth . . . a section of about ten acres of low, flat land [at] the mouth of this river was entirely submerged for some minutes immediately after the shock." Point Arena marks the spot where the San Andreas Fault runs out to sea.

• *November 4, 1927.* This is the best-documented tsunami of local origin in the history of California and was probably caused by an offshore earthquake. A five-foot-high wave was recorded at Port San Luis and a six-foot wave at nearby Surf.

• *Good Friday, 1964.* The tsunami from the Alaskan Good Friday earthquake caused millions of dollars in damage along the California shore, especially at Crescent City, just south of the Oregon border. Here is how one report on the Crescent City disaster described the waves:

> As the first wave moved into the city, bringing logs and debris with it, the water rose rapidly with the small waves riding the crest. Front street was covered in places with . . . water and logs which partially blocked traffic. . . . The second and third waves seemed of lesser magnitude than the first and to hit with less force. But the fourth wave was fast in rising; it hit the city hardest, such that it left in its wake a large area of total destruction. . . . When this wave receded, cars, refrigerators, gas tanks, and debris of all sorts floated toward the sea. It was this highest wave that was responsible for . . . twelve dead.

The 1964 tsunami caused more than $12 million in damage along the California coast (in 1983 dollars). Most of the damage occurred in Crescent City, where fifty-four houses were destroyed and thirty-seven others damaged. One hundred fifty businesses in Crescent City either were wiped out or sustained heavy damage. Some houses were lifted off their foundations by the wave and came to rest in the street. Other structures were smashed by the logs and automobiles carried along by the wave; moving at perhaps thirty miles per hour, these heavy objects became, in effect, waterborne battering rams. Fifteen boats were capsized in the harbor at Crescent City, and a dock was damaged severely, by the wave itself and by a barge that was slammed into the dock.

Other communities along the California shore were also hit badly by the tsunami. A U.S. Coast and Geodetic Survey report summarizes part of the damage to places south of Crescent City:

> [In] Mendocino County . . . approximately one hundred fishing boats in Noyo Harbor suffered damage, with ten being sunk. A dredge in the harbor was carried upstream about one-fourth mile and grounded on a sandbar. Estimates of the damage ranged from $250,000 to $1 million. In Marin County, approximately $1 million worth of damage was done to small boats and berthing facilities, mostly in Loch Lomond Harbor in San Rafael. Los Angeles County Civil Defense reported $100,000 to $200,000 damage to six small-boat slips, pilings, and [a] fuel dock; $75,000 damage due to scouring action on the harbor sides in Los Angeles County Harbor; and eight docks with a value of $100,000 destroyed in Long Beach Harbor.

Thus far, the southern California coast has been lucky. It seems less prone to devastating, locally generated tsunamis than the shores of Japan or Alaska. (Visitors to southeastern Alaska are sometimes surprised to see, posted on the doors of their hotel rooms, detailed instructions on what to do in case a tsunami hits.) Moreover, tsunami damage in California has been minor compared with earthquake damage on land. Between 1812 and 1975, onshore quake damage in California was more than one hundred times greater than tsunami damage along the shores.

This is not to say, however, that very large tsunamis from quakes in southern California are impossible, or that the danger from such waves should be ignored. McCullough admits that "a preliminary appraisal of the potential for locally generated tsunamis suggests that wave run-up heights as great as four to six meters," or about thirteen to twenty feet, could be caused by faulting on the seabed. Wave run-up heights of perhaps ten feet might be expected for seismically active areas farther south. Waves like these are not in the same category

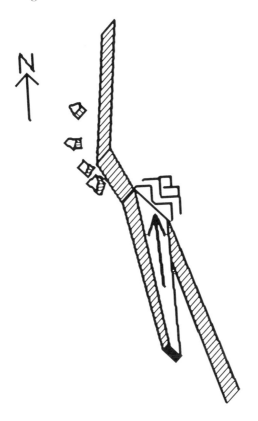

Southern California's "Earthquake Machine": This idealized diagram shows Baja California moving northward and grinding against southern California, pushing up the Transverse Ranges (center) in the process. Small "slivers" of crustal rock are ground away and make their way slowly around the bend of the southern California coast. The instability of these slivers causes earthquakes. *(Courtesy of Allan Frank)*

with the giant tsunamis that hit Hawaii in 1946 and 1975, but even a five- or six-foot tsunami can cause widespread damage in a harbor or along any other densely settled stretch of coastline.

One tsunami-prone area in southern California is located off Santa Barbara. Here and in the offshore area near Point Arguello to the west, an odd set of conditions has created the potential for making large seismic sea waves.

Some of the geologic structures in the Transverse Ranges (the mountains that run roughly crosswise to the shore) cut diagonally across the strike-slip faults near the coast and run out to sea near Santa Barbara. These structures are experiencing what geologists call *compressive tectonic deformation.* That is, they are being squeezed out of shape by the powerful forces pressing on them.

This deformation process creates up-and-down movement: in geological language, *dip-slip displacement.* To see how this movement might generate tsunamis, let us imagine that the water off the California coast and the sediments on the bottom are completely transparent, so that you could see all the way to the fractured bedrock below.

On the bottom you would see two long, narrow bunches of fault lines. The one near the shore is called the Hosgri Fault Zone and is made up of about two dozen small faults running roughly parallel to the coast. About twenty miles to the southwest lies another heavily fractured patch of seabed, the Santa Lucia Bank. The faults here, too, run more or less parallel to the shore.

Both fault zones are under pressure from the westward-pushing crustal fragments that are trying to "turn the corner" around the southern tip of the mountains, as described in chapter 2. Shoved thus from the east, what can the little chunks of crust in these fault zones do?

They cannot slide north or south to get out of the way because they are locked in place by firm, unbroken crust on those two sides. And westward movement is impossible because the huge Pacific plate blocks the way. The crustal fragments in the fault zones are literally caught between a rock and a hard place.

That leaves only one way to move: vertically. So from time to time a chunk of one of those fault zones pops up or dips down, under the relentless pressure from the east. The result is an earthquake with vertical displacement.

On land, that would be the end of the event. A hunk of rock would rise or fall slightly, and that would be all. But conditions are different at the bottom of the sea because the water above the fault zones is incompressible. Consequently, if part of the seabed rises or falls suddenly, the water over it will rise or fall, too, by a corresponding amount. Should the movement on the seabed be big enough, it will cause a tsunami.

So the fault zones offshore near Santa Barbara are potential tsunami makers. In view of the fact that this part of the California coast has the highest rates of uplift (that is, vertical movement), both short term and long term, people living around Santa Barbara might be excused for looking nervously at the ocean now and then.

As one report on southern California's tsunami potential puts it, "Surface fault rupture accompanied by sea-floor displacement is a distinct possibility beneath Santa Barbara Channel." To put it another way, a big quake on land could set off another quake under the sea and thus send tsunamis rolling toward the southern California shore.

How often do earthquakes under the channel create tsunamis? The historical record is spotty, but one estimate puts the interval between big tsunamis in this part of California at about 135 years. Yet this is little more than a guess. California may not have its next great tsunami for another fifty years—or the wave might roll over the beaches next week. We simply cannot say when it will occur or how big and destructive the wave will be.

A tsunami's size depends on the magnitude of the earthquake that causes it, as well as many other factors. A quake that registered about 7.0 on the Richter scale, under the right circumstances, would probably generate a tsunami big enough to be hazardous. The wave would damage boats at their moorings and might run several feet vertically up the beach: enough to cause substantial destruction at numerous settlements along the coast and take a few dozen lives by sweeping away unwary bathers and by overturning boats.

But now let us consider what will happen in a much more powerful earthquake. What will the offshore faults do if a true superquake hits Los Angeles? Will they remain quiet, or will they respond with tsunamigenic (tsunami-making) violence of their own?

As a rule geologists are cautious and conservative about making such predictions, but they admit that almost anything should be considered possible in the next superquake, if only because we have so little experience with such disasters.

There is another way—besides vertical movement along offshore faults—for a submarine earthquake to create tsunamis along the southern California coast. The quake might set off submarine landslides, which in turn could generate tsunamis.

Landslides on the seabed, known to geologists as *turbidity flows,* are much like slides on dry land. In places, the offshore slope is so steep that a quake may dislodge a slab of sediment near the shore and send it slipping down the gradient, largely intact. The initial slippage itself could cause a tsunami by suddenly leaving a cavity in the seabed where the upper edge of the slab once rested. The ocean surface would dip downward, then rebound, creating a wave that would ripple out in all directions and strike the nearby shore.

A second, bigger wave would probably result when the moving hunk of sediment finally halted. The "toe," or leading edge, of the sediment block would tip upward as it came to rest, making water bulge upward on the surface and thus creating another tsunami. U.S. Geological Survey studies have concluded that sediments off the southern California coast have the potential to cause tsunamis this way, though the danger is not considered excessive.

Still another factor may play a role in generating tsunamis: methane outbursts, as described in chapter 2. Here we enter the realm of speculation, for there is no proof that a methane eruption from the sea floor has ever generated more than a few small ripples. But let us perform an experiment in our imaginations to see how tsunamis and methane eruptions may be linked.

Suppose a quake is accompanied by a huge methane eruption from the seabed. Giant bubbles of gas rise from the ocean floor and head for the surface. As they climb, the bubbles make water pile up on top of them. Just before they burst, they are covered momentarily by great domes of water. Then, *whoom:* the bubbles rupture, the water domes collapse, and the resulting disturbance sends tsunamis on their way to neighboring coastlines.

The bursting of very large methane bubbles at sea would release great amounts of energy but might not necessarily be associated with major earthquakes. This hypothesis may explain why some relatively minor earthquakes are accompanied by large tsunamis and why tsunamis sometimes appear seemingly out of nowhere, when no strong quakes are anywhere in evidence.

But tsunamis, if they occur at all, are liable to be a mere sideshow in the coming California superquake. Most of the damage will be on land—and to better understand the imminent danger facing southern California, let us now look closely at the geology of Los Angeles and its environs.

4

Los Angeles: The Earthquake City

ngelenos call Los Angeles "the city of the angels." Perhaps it is better described as a city of paradoxes. Metropolitan Los Angeles, spread out over an area bigger than Rhode Island, is so huge and populous that almost anything one says about it is likely to be true—and the opposite to be true as well. Los Angeles is rich and poor, progressive and reactionary, lovely and hideous, carnal and spiritual. It is the wealth of Malibu and the poverty of Watts. It is the accumulated wisdom in the UCLA library and the blind faith of worshipers at storefront churches. It is clean beaches and filthy air. Los Angeles is almost anything one can imagine, and its antithesis at the same time. Founded by Spanish missionaries as an outpost of God's kingdom, it became a mighty monument to worldly power and pleasure. And while Los Angeles is scorned in the East as a symbol of everything crass and tasteless, the city has the West's greatest concentration of first-class universities, museums, and other intellectual and cultural facilities.

Driving through Los Angeles is like no other experience. It lets you sample virtually the whole history of the West, and almost every major culture on earth, on a single tank of gas. A few minutes' drive will take you from sedate, down-to-earth

Burbank to arty Venice, or from a downtown museum full of Renaissance paintings to the aerospace firms near Bakersfield, where the technology of the next century is taking shape today. Los Angeles is a great agglomeration of individuals with frontier traits—ingenuity, strength, buoyancy, exuberance—all working to push their city and the world toward their particular visions of the future. Look at Los Angeles today, and you may very well be looking at the world of tomorrow.

On a clear day, from a tall building downtown, you can see from the San Gabriel Mountains in the east to the blue Pacific in the west, and on an exceptionally smog-free day, the offshore islands are visible in the distance. (These islands, like the land under Los Angeles itself, are bits of crustal debris that flew off, as from a lathe, during Baja California's slow collision with the mountains to its north.) No sight in southern California is more beautiful and exotic than Los Angeles—unless it is a geologic map of the area.

The state of California publishes geologic maps that are also breathtaking works off art. Splashed across the map of Los Angeles are blobs of color that look like something out of Dali, with touches of Matisse and Klee. Pasadena shows up bright tangerine, with a pattern of small gray dots indicating nonmarine sediment or soil blown in on the wind or carried down from the nearby San Gabriel Mountains. Those mountains are a study in glowing pink (Mesozoic granite, from the age of dinosaurs) and various shades of brown (Precambrian granite, probably older than life itself). If a cat sat down on this map, its rump would cover formations spanning perhaps half a billion years, from mud deposited just last week to granite that solidified long before the first living things arose. The geology of Los Angeles is just as multiverse and fascinating as the city.

The place names on the map are an entertaining study in themselves. Mount Disappointment. Mount Harvard. Loggerhead Mountain. Big Chief Mine. There is even a sound of romance in the names of the rock formations, such as Pelona schist.

Through the mountains on this map run thick black lines that indicate faults. Some of them have prosaic names: Holser Fault, Northridge Hill Fault, Transmission Line Fault. Others have names to conjure with, such as Magic Mountain Fault.

The San Andreas Fault is unmistakable. It slashes across the map, dividing Antelope Valley from Angeles National Forest. Much less conspicuous is the Inglewood Fault, a thin dotted line running off the bottom of the map past the Baldwin Hills Reservoir. Remember the Inglewood Fault, however, for it is dangerous out of all proportion to its size, as we shall see shortly.

Over wide areas of the map spread pale yellow blotches, the color of lemon sherbet. This marks alluvium, the stuff that streams lay down. We will refer to alluvium again in a later chapter because it caused serious damage from liquefaction in the 1971 San Fernando earthquake and is expected to do so again in Los Angeles's impending earthquake.

The San Fernando earthquake is one of the most famous of this century. Its fame is not due to its magnitude. It registered only 6.6 on the Richter scale or less than a hundredth the rating of the 1906 San Francisco quake. Seismologists consider the San Fernando quake a moderate earthquake, of the kind that occurs somewhere in California roughly every five years.

What made the San Fernando quake special was that it occurred in a densely populated urban area and demonstrated, as no amount of laboratory analysis ever could, how ill prepared California is for the coming superquake.

The San Fernando earthquake killed 64 persons, injured approximately 2,400, and caused an estimated half billion dollars in property damage alone. In addition to this gross wreckage, the earthquake created countless lesser difficulties in the Los Angeles area. For example:

- The quake caused a temporary judicial log jam. Courts in Los Angeles, Burbank, Van Nuys, and San Fernando were shut down because of damage or power failure.
- Tap water turned brackish in the San Fernando Valley immediately after the quake, and bottled water was the only alternative for drinking. Sellers of bottled water did a land-office business.
- Owners of gas stoves could not simply turn their burners back on after gas service was restored following the quake. The pilot lights had to be reignited by servicemen.
- Schools had to be closed for damage inspection.

- Elevators halted between floors in areas where power was cut off. One woman spent three and a half hours in a court-house elevator before being rescued.
- Libraries had a mammoth cleanup job. The central public library in downtown Los Angeles was especially hard hit; thousands of books were shaken off the shelves. The situation was worst in the religion and philosophy room, where books lay piled in heaps three feet high.
- Cal Tech's switchboard was deluged with calls from frantic Angelenos when a rumor started circulating that campus scientists had predicted another strong earthquake for that day. The university denied the rumor.

Humans were not the only victims of the earthquake. Animal shelters were flooded with four-footed refugees. In Los Angeles, one shelter had to make room for seventy-five dogs and cats left homeless by the disaster. Another shelter had a more exotic mix of guests, including several pet monkeys, squirrels, chipmunks, and sheep. One hundred forty-one guinea pigs were evacuated from a hospital laboratory. Perhaps most urgent of all was the plight of some fifty thousand chickens at an egg farm. The birds needed water, but the quake had cut off water supplies. The city found a way to save them: every day, a street-sweeping vehicle stopped by the ranch and refreshed the birds with water from its tank.

The earthquake had its lighter side. Local papers reported numerous amusing human-interest stories in the days following the tremor. For example:

- Hansen Dam Lake had been stocked with trout and opened to the public for fishing three months earlier. The San Fernando incident proved that it takes more than an earthquake to stop a dedicated angler, for several fishermen showed up immediately after the quake, gear in hand. One of the anglers told the *Los Angeles Times* he "figured the quake would jolt some of the big ones from the bottom."
- Downtown, an operator at the city's golf reservation system was trying to keep her seat in the swaying building when a call came through from Van Nuys. "I know how things are," the caller said, "but I just have to get in my reservation for Saturday."
- Liquor merchants in Newhall lost much of their stock as

the quake knocked bottles off shelves. The only way to deal with the mess was to sweep up the shattered glass, then wash the spilled wine and liquor into the gutters with a hose. "All anyone would have needed," one reporter noted, "was a straw."

But most accounts of the quake's effects were grim. Granada Hills suffered heavily. *Times* reporter Ken Lubas, who lived in the neighborhood, contributed an eyewitness report. He and his wife were awakened by a roar, the noise of shattering glass, and S-waves that sent their bed "crashing into an opposite wall." Getting up and looking around the house, they found virtually everything inside either upset or broken. Outside, their neighbors were standing on the sidewalk, some of them still in their bedclothes. Beyond, Lubas could see houses starting to catch fire in the nearby hills.

The couple left their house. The street looked "weird," Lubas recalled. Fallen bricks lay far from the houses of which they once were part, and the pavement was buckled and fissured where the S-waves had passed through.

A few minutes later Lubas was driving through Los Angeles with his cameras to record the damage on film. Aftershocks were rocking the city, and occasionally Lubas saw a pedestrian hanging on to a lamppost for support as the ground shook underfoot. Lubas passed a handsome house that he and his wife had considered buying when they were newlyweds. Now it was ablaze. Neighbors were hosing down their roofs to prevent the fire from spreading.

Driving was hazardous for Lubas at times because live telephone wires had been shaken down by the continuing aftershocks. Indeed, driving was impossible in some areas where the tremor had demolished highways. The Golden State Freeway was "a mess," Lubas recalled. A new overpass had fallen and blocked the lanes in both directions.

Making his way through the business district of San Fernando, Lubas found its streets littered with broken glass and brick. He had to avoid large fissures that had opened in the ground and skirt some minor floods where broken mains were gushing water.

The heaviest hit of all local communities was Sylmar, at the foot of the San Gabriel Mountains. The *Los Angeles Times* opened a news story about the damage this way: "Sylmar Wednesday appeared as if a huge hand had reached down, picked up the entire community, and given it a terrible shaking. . . . Many houses and businesses were without windows, chimneys, roofs, and walls; streets were buckled; power lines were down; and there was no water, gas, electricity, or telephone service."

The strength of ground motions in the San Fernando quake could be seen clearly near the intersection of Wallaby and Rajah streets in Sylmar. The ground here was literally shattered by the quake. For about two hundred feet atop a ridge running parallel to Wallaby Street, the earth was broken and overturned, looking as if it had just been plowed for planting.

So thoroughly churned was the soil that, after the quake, 90 percent of the earth consisted of fresh mineral soil brought up from underground. Only 10 percent was made of grassy tops of soil clods. If this phenomenon seems unimpressive, imagine doing the same job yourself to a suburban lawn. Then imagine doing the whole job in less than sixty seconds. That is how fierce the ground motions were in Sylmar.

Exactly how the "plowing" effect occurred, and why it was confined to the top of one ridge in Sylmar, scientists are unsure. The quake had little or no effect on the slopes of the ridge. So far, the best explanation is that an *interference effect* caused the damage.

Interference effects are just what their name indicates: situations that result when wave patterns encounter and interfere with one another. You may have seen interference effects at work on the beach, where two wave systems come together. Depending on the characteristics of the wave systems, they may cancel each other out entirely, leaving flat, glossy stretches of water, or they may reinforce each other, making big waves where before there were only little ones.

Now substitute earthquake waves for waves in the sea, and it is easy to see how that ridge crest in Sylmar might have been sifted and overturned. Possibly the ridge acted as a lens, focusing two sets of S-waves into the same place at the same time, with dramatic consequences. The lesson of this little upheaval on Wallaby Street is that quake vibrations are unpredictable things, and it is impossible to say just how S-waves will behave. At places one never expects, they may come together, perform a little dance with one another, and leave behind a bizarre testimonial to the power of an earthquake, as they did just off one little street in Sylmar.

An intriguing sidelight on the San Fernando quake was an incident that took place off Malibu Point in the hours just after dawn. (Malibu Point lies about thirty miles southwest of the quake's epicenter, so it was largely unaffected except for minor structural damage to some homes.) As the morning fog burned away, observers on shore saw the waters bubbling vigorously about a quarter mile from the mouth of Malibu Creek. The bubbling was noticed around 8:00 A.M. but is believed to have started about the same time as the earthquake, approximately 6:00 A.M.

Bubbles were rising to the surface in two places, where the water was twenty to twenty-five feet deep. Gradually the bubbling action diminished, but gas bubbles about an inch wide were still rising to the surface in large numbers when a team of U.S. Geological Survey researchers arrived at the scene two days later for a look at this odd phenomenon. There was only one way to conduct a close-up study of the gas release: go to the seabed for a look. So several of the geologists donned diving equipment and went down.

They found an unattractive landscape waiting for them underwater. The sea floor off Malibu is covered with brown sand mixed with large amounts of organic debris, which generates a fetid smell when brought to the surface. The divers looked for signs of undersea damage from the quake, but there were none. Here, as on land at Malibu, the quake had not been strong enough to rupture or dislocate the ground. Artifacts such as anchor chains were lying clearly undisturbed on the sand.

But an interesting sight awaited the divers. Here and there the bottom was pocked with clusters of craters, almost like the surface of the moon. These craters were the source of the mysterious bubbles. Clearly the gas bubbles had been released from underground.

What were the bubbles made of? Were they ordinary air that had somehow been trapped undersea and set free when the earthquake shook them loose? Or had they an entirely different composition?

Finding out was easy. All the divers had to do was collect a few samples, by inverting glass containers filled with water over the streams of bubbles, then sealing the containers. The samples were brought ashore and sent to Washington, D.C., for chemical analysis.

The analysis was about what devotees of the deep gas hypothesis would expect. After water vapor was removed from the samples, they turned out to be 93 percent pure methane. The rest of the samples consisted (in decreasing order) of nitrogen, carbon dioxide, oxygen, and argon.

Does this mean the deep gas hypothesis is correct? Did the San Fernando quake release hydrocarbons that had been cooking deep inside the earth since our planet was formed from cosmic debris billions of years ago?

Not necessarily. There are other possible sources for the methane. It may have been formed by decaying organic material in the sediment and jiggled loose by the shock of the quake. (On land, methane is commonly formed by decaying plant matter in swamps and marshes. This is why methane is sometimes called *swamp gas* or *marsh gas*.) It seems unlikely that the gas was released from oil fields near Los Angeles, because natural gas (which is mostly methane) from those fields contains substantial amounts of other hydrocarbons, ethane and propane, which were not found in the samples collected off Malibu. So the Malibu bubbles, while tantalizing, did not resolve the controversy over the deep gas hypothesis. That scientific fight will probably continue for years to come.

Perhaps the most widely publicized effect of the San Fernando earthquake was the wreckage of Olive View Hospital, an 880-bed facility owned by Los Angeles County. One official report on the earthquake described the situation at Olive View in the following words:

> Power failed, communications were out, four stair towers were out, elevators were inoperative, and the hospital was on the verge of collapse. No panic ensued, and patients were successfully evacuated to other hospitals. Three lives were lost; two [died] when power failed and the electrically operated life support systems stopped, and the third life loss occurred when a person . . . attempting to leave the building was struck by a collapsing portion of the building.

Fortunately, the report added, "the time of day (6:01 A.M.) found very few or no persons in the first story, basement, and stair towers. Life loss would have been significantly higher had the earthquake occurred later in the day."

The heart of the hospital was its medical treatment and care building, a five-story structure built of reinforced concrete and completed in 1970, only a few months before the earthquake. Though it appeared to be a single unit, the structure was actually five buildings in one, counting four towers containing stairs and dayroom areas. These towers were separated about four inches from the main building and were held in place by reinforced concrete columns.

The columns failed during the quake, and all four towers came loose from the main building. Three of them toppled over completely, while the fourth merely leaned a bit to the north. Each of the dislodged towers was as big as a small office building. That gives you some idea of the forces that shook Olive View that February morning.

Part of the first story was crushed when the south stair tower dropped on it. The carport gave way and fell on several ambulances. Outside the emergency entrance, several precast concrete wall panels broke loose from their supporting structures and came crashing down. "Collapse nearly occurred" in the rest of the first story, the report went on, because the earthquake caused the entire building to lean about two feet northward. Had its slant been a bit more pronounced, the upper portion of the building would have fallen on and flattened the entire first floor. A total collapse did not occur in part because of the strength of the reinforced concrete columns on the first floor; though badly damaged by the temblor, they retained enough strength to hold up the building.

Inspectors who dared to venture into the building following the quake found a scene of almost total destruction. The floor was covered with fallen ceiling tile. Windows that once stood vertical now leaned inward at about a ten-degree angle. Elevator doors were jammed shut, and the front door was racked into a rhomboidal pattern. In the basement, telephone switching equipment was twisted and scattered in heaps all over the floor. Steel reinforcing bars in the concrete had snapped like toothpicks.

Outside, the reinforced concrete columns on the first-floor

level had shattered almost like glass. Their outer layer of concrete had disintegrated and fallen to the ground, while the concrete cores of the columns had fragmented into large chunks that were held inside, like caged animals, by twisted vertical reinforcing rods. Nearby, the quake had overturned concrete benches—any one of which was too heavy for a person to tilt—and knocked the concrete canopy of an outdoor walkway several degrees off the vertical.

This building, remember, was brand new and supposed to be quake-resistant. Older structures at Olive View fared much worse. The psychiatric building, also thought to be resistant to earthquakes, was virtually wiped out. Its first story had collapsed totally. The destruction of this building was of special interest to seismologists and engineers because of how gradually it had collapsed. Several persons were on the second floor when the earthquake struck, and they described the settling of the building as remarkably gentle.

Here again, a Fire Safety Ratings Bureau report pointed out, "the time of day proved to be most fortunate." On a normal day, about 300 persons would have been in the collapsed first story, and many of them would have been killed if the earthquake had occurred during working hours.

Even when some buildings themselves at Olive View rode out the earthquake well, their contents did not. In the central heating and air conditioning plant, which itself was relatively unhurt (only about 20 percent damage), heavy equipment was tossed around like a child's playthings. Boilers were knocked four feet out of position. Weighty batteries, used to activate standby power operation, fell off storage shelves and crashed to the floor. Overhead pipes as thick as a man's thigh snapped a foot or more out of alignment, while an emergency generator was ripped off its mountings.

Though most of Olive View was still standing after the earthquake, damage was so extensive—even to some new, supposedly quake-resistant parts of the facility—that the hospital was practically a total loss. Some damage was inevitable because many portions of the hospital were more than fifty years old, but the virtual destruction of Olive View came as a surprise to Angelenos who thought all their local medical care facilities would be available to care for casualties following a major quake.

At first glance it looked as if horizontal shear waves were responsible for the destruction at Olive View. Soil near the hospital was tortured much like the soil near Wallaby Street. Pavement was shattered. Fissures were observed in the ground. Heavy concrete benches were knocked over. All these features are associated with strong horizontal ground motion.

But in fact much of the damage was due to vertical ground motion—that is, a violent up-and-down shaking. "Excessive vertical forces" accounted for a large part of the ruin at Olive View, especially the destruction of first-floor columns at the main building, the fire safety report concluded. Rough calculations carried out after the quake put its vertical ground motion at approximately .67 g, or two-thirds the normal force of gravity. A person bouncing on a trampoline experiences g-forces in that same range. So in effect, the San Fernando earthquake gave an entire hospital complex the equivalent of a trampoline ride.

All things considered, Olive View got off easy. Only three persons were killed, and most structures remained more or less intact. Damage was many times worse at the Veterans Hospital at the foot of the San Gabriel Mountains by Pacoima Canyon. Forty-seven persons, the majority of the quake's fatalities, were killed here, and much of the Veterans Hospital complex collapsed entirely.

Reverend Edward McHugh, a Catholic chaplain, was leaving the chapel and on his way to wards housing cardiac and respiratory patients when the earthquake hit. He was thrown to the ground about sixty feet from the building and looked back at the chapel just in time to see it crumble. "Thank God I wasn't in there," he told the press afterward.

Two women working in a basement kitchen at the hospital were less lucky than Reverend McHugh. They were trapped for hours under the rubble of a collapsed building before rescuers succeeded in digging them out. A baker at the hospital kitchen was also buried under rubble. He saved himself by diving under a sink, which shielded him from falling debris. There he sat for the next fifty-eight hours, while a team of volunteers, including his brother-in-law, dug through the fallen brick and plaster in search of him. Finally they heard his voice, and a few minutes later he was free, with no more injuries than a broken hand and wrist and a few bruises.

A large part of the Veterans Hospital was built before 1933, the year the Long Beach earthquake inspired the California legislature to mandate stiffer building requirements for quake-proofing buildings. Ironically, several years before the 1971 earthquake, officials had decided the hospital buildings were so sturdy that all they needed was a mere renovation.

Possibly the most chilling of all harm done by the quake was the damage to the Lower San Fernando Dam, one of a complex of three dams in the hills. Part of the Lower San Fernando Dam collapsed into the reservoir behind it, reducing the *free-board*, or space between the top of the dam and the water level behind it, to little more than the length of a man's arm. The dam came within a narrow margin of failing and releasing a flood on eighty thousand residents of the valley downstream.

Here is how a Division of Safety of Dams report described the damage:

> The Lower San Fernando Dam experienced the worst damage of all the dams in the complex. The . . . parapet wall, dam crest, most of the upstream slope, and a portion of the downstream slope, for a length of about 1,800 feet, slid into the reservoir. As much as 800,000 cubic yards of dam embankment may have been displaced into the reservoir, resulting in a loss of about thirty feet of dam height. . . .
>
> Shortly after the major damage to the dam had been assessed, several hundred sandbags were filled and stored on the downstream slope. . . . These were made ready for use in the event that aftershocks would bring about a significant decrease in the minimum freeboard remaining. Because of the critically reduced freeboard, the uncertain degree of damage to the Upper San Fernando Dam, and the possibility of strong aftershocks, residents in [the] area below the dam were evacuated. . . .
>
> The east outlet tower was cracked at the base and broken off about twenty feet above the base, and came to rest in an upstream orientation. The sliding earth fill and concrete slope paving covered the remaining upright stem of the tower and blocked the opening to the

outlet conduit, temporarily restricting flow through this outlet. . . .

The report goes on to say: "Eighty thousand . . . people living downstream of the dam were immediately ordered to evacuate, and steps were taken to lower the water level in the reservoir as rapidly as possible. This was successfully accomplished. . . . However, the margin by which a major disaster was averted was uncomfortably small. If the city had not been operating the reservoir at a water level lower than normal, if the earthquake shaking had continued for a few seconds longer, or if the Upper San Fernando Dam, which moved downstream six feet during the earthquake, had released additional water into the reservoir, overtopping of the remaining embankment could have occurred." Here, *overtopping* means a spill of water over the shattered rim of the dam—in effect, a flood.

The report says more about damage to the Upper San Fernando Dam:

> The quake damaged the Upper San Fernando Dam by a general movement downstream and a slumping in elevation. The dam crest moved about five feet downstream [six feet is the figure cited elsewhere in the report] and settled about three feet vertically. The upstream concrete slope paving was displaced and damaged. . . . The dam was drawn down quickly . . . then continued in operation to provide aqueduct water into the city's system. The outlet tower remained upright, although experiencing considerable damage. The outlet line from the tower was severely affected by the dam's movement, and several openings developed. . . .

Quick action prevented further damage, as the survey reports:

> Shortly after the main shock, it was discovered that very muddy water was issuing from the downstream toe of the dam. This water appeared to be coming from around the outside of the old outlet line, which was in use. After the gates in the outlet tower were closed along with a gate downstream in the outlet line, and the

pressure taken off this portion of the line between the tower and the closed gate by opening two blow-off valves, the flow at the toe of the dam dropped to an insignificant rate . . . and cleared up considerably. These valve operations stopped possible serious erosion of the dam. . . .

The Lower San Fernando Dam was not a solid concrete structure, as some other U.S. dams are, but rather a huge, scientifically designed pile of earth. It was built largely of "a potpourri of wagon-dumped and rolled fills," stated a Division of Safety of Dams report after the earthquake. Such a structure fairly begged to be liquefied. Only chance—and the quick response of a few employees on the site—prevented tremendous destruction and loss of life.

Press coverage of the dam's narrow escape seldom mentioned that another dam fifty miles north of Los Angeles—the San Francisquito Dam on the Santa Clara River—did fail in a 1928 earthquake, sending a flood raging down the valley and killing between 400 and 450 persons.

The San Francisquito disaster began a few minutes before midnight on March 12, 1928. A quake shook the hills around the dam, sending rock slides cascading down the slopes. Five miles downstream from the dam at Powerhouse No. 2, a six-story concrete structure housing generating equipment and accommodations for technicians and their families, the walls started shaking, and windows rattled. The quake grew stronger. Lights at the powerhouse dimmed, then went out altogether as the dam collapsed.

In Los Angeles the disaster showed up as a brief flicker of the city's lights. Attendants at power receiving stations saw voltage dip sharply for about two seconds. At one substation, a transmission line shorted out, and an oil switch exploded. Technicians rushed to repair the switch, unaware of the catastrophe taking place a few miles away.

Five minutes later after the dam failed, a wall of reservoir water more than one hundred feet high rolled over the powerhouse and crushed it. There were only three survivors from Powerhouse No. 2; twenty-five others in the building were killed. Powerhouse No. 1, above the dam, was spared.

The water rolled down the valley at a leisurely pace—only

about six miles per hour. But what it lacked in velocity, it made up for in destructive power, for it picked up thousands of tons of rock, steel, and other debris, adding its terrific energy to that of the water.

The flood submerged the Saticoy Bridge, but the structure survived. Four miles downstream, the old wooden Montalvo Bridge lost two hundred feet of its span. A railroad bridge nearby survived largely intact but lost a section of track on one side.

As it neared the ocean, the water spread out over the flood-plain until at one point it was two miles wide. The flood missed Oxnard, but officials there took no chances; as soon as they received word of the disaster upstream, they had the community evacuated. When the sun rose that morning, the people of Oxnard saw the deluge, with its burden of trees and homes and assorted debris, rolling in a vast gray stream toward the sea and the offshore islands.

The San Francisquito disaster was quickly forgotten—partly because the tragedy was too painful to relive and partly because Los Angeles's collective memory is short: any event more than forty years old is ancient history. Even memories of the 1971 earthquake have faded in Los Angeles, so Angelenos seem to have relapsed into a false sense of security. But merely dismissing a danger will not dispel it; and in the near future, the Los Angeles area will suffer a severe shaking, with calamitous results. What follows is a projection of what Angelenos may expect on earthquake day.

5

Earthquake Day

The time is 7:30 on a summer morning in a year not too far distant. The place is Los Angeles, and the occasion is the most destructive earthquake in twentieth-century American history.

After the next few minutes have passed, Los Angeles will never look the same again. So let us take a quick overview of the metropolitan area in the last moments before the superquake.

The whole city is in motion. Even at this early hour the freeways are full of traffic as commuters flock into Los Angeles from their homes in the suburbs. Motorists zoom along elevated highways, scarcely realizing that they and the roads are supported by a delicate balance of gravitation and structural bracing. That balance will be upset shortly, with catastrophic effect.

On the streets of the city itself, buses wind their way through traffic. Moving vans lug the belongings of householders from one home to another. Tank trucks haul their liquid cargoes—water, milk, gasoline, ammonia, liquid oxygen, propane, and dozens of other substances—inside thin-skinned receptacles. Some of these trucks are, in effect, rolling bombs. Others are full of elements and compounds so dangerous that their use in combat might constitute a violation of the articles of war.

Rail lines snaking through the city carry dangerous cargoes of their own. One tank car is clearly marked LIQUID CHLORINE. Another bears the label FORMALDEHYDE. Still another is filled with a nitrite that, on exposure to air, would form an airborne cloud of nitric acid mist. Other cargoes are nontoxic but highly flammable: lumber from the northwestern forests, coal from the Rockies, paper from Canada.

At the airport, planes arrive and depart at intervals of perhaps two minutes. Their safe takeoff and landing—at speeds exceeding 150 miles per hour—are predicted on the assumption that the ground beneath the runway will remain reasonably still. Most of the time that assumption holds true. Today it will not.

Not all travelers are in cars or on aircraft. Many are riding bicycles or skating to work. A small army of skateboarders rolls along the boardwalks near the ocean, while joggers wearing headphones pound along the pavement to the strains of Vivaldi or rock.

Even underground, Los Angeles is in constant movement. Water for the city is rushing in from the east through subterranean pipes; natural gas flows through mains in every corner of the metropolis; and electrons shoot back and forth through buried phone lines, carrying the communications on which the city's life depends.

This is, in short, a typical summer morning for Los Angeles. The weather is slightly warmer than usual, and a smog alert is in effect, too. Los Angeles' notorious atmospheric inversion is at work again, trapping pollutants in the air just above the city. Radio announcers warn L.A. residents to stay indoors and avoid unnecessary exertion if they have respiratory trouble, because hazardous air-quality conditions are expected to continue for at least the next forty-eight hours. The announcers add that smokers in the hills near the city should be careful where they toss cigarette butts, for an unusually dry summer has left the woods and fields susceptible to fire. Several times in recent years, accidental fires have run wild in the hills around Los Angeles and consumed millions of dollars in property; only the prompt response of fire crews has prevented whole subdivisions from going up in smoke. No one likes to think what might happen if a fire started on this hot, bone-dry day.

Household pets are suffering from the heat. Unknown to many of their owners, the animals are also troubled by something else: the faint, subsonic rumblings—inaudible to humans but perceptible to the keener senses of other species—that precede a major earthquake. Dogs and cats scratch at doors, demanding to be let outside, while birds twitter nervously in their cages.

Looking over the city from the top of a downtown skyscraper, an observer would see one of the world's greatest cities preparing to start a typical workday. But a viewer with the power to see through rock would realize that this is not a typical day. To the northeast, the crust along the Newport-Inglewood Fault is getting ready to move.

The Newport-Inglewood Fault is hardly a household word, even in the communities it underlies. It is only a few miles long: hardly in the same category as the lordly San Andreas to the east. Indeed, the Newport-Inglewood Fault is not a single fault at all, but a string of several short faults—the Inglewood Fault, Potrero Fault, and so forth—laid approximately end to end through the heart of metropolitan Los Angeles. Altogether these faults are known to geologists as the "Newport-Inglewood Fault Zone." But their small size and seeming disunity makes them no less dangerous, for they run straight down the middle of the biggest population center in the western states. They stretch under Long Beach, continue northwest between Hawthorne Lawn and Huntington Park, skirt a patch of exposed bedrock in Culver City, and come to an end just east of Santa Monica.

Virtually the entire Los Angeles metropolitan area lies within five miles in either direction of the Newport-Inglewood Fault Zone. Venice, with its distinctive canals and expensive waterfront property; Hollywood, where quakes have inspired more than a few motion pictures; Santa Monica, that enclave of militant liberalism—these and several dozen more communities lie almost within shouting distance of the fault zone. Some are right on top of it; others are only a mile or two distant. An S-wave can cover a mile in about the time it takes to say "earthquake."

For years the rock on either side of the fault zone has been stretching out of shape as the crustal mass approaching from the south has tried to slip around the southern end of the San Gabriel Mountains. The movement has not been smooth. The rock has "stuck" along the fault; strain has reached the breaking point; and the only thing that can relieve it is a break, in the form of a powerful earthquake.

There is no warning.

At universities and other research centers all over the western United States and Canada, needles on seismographs start to quiver. The needles swing in wider and wider arcs, until the paper under them is practically black with the wavy marks that indicate the superquake has arrived.

But it is not quite the quake the experts expected. The scientists had wagered that the big quake, when it came, would originate on the San Andreas Fault. And that seemed a wise bet, for the San Andreas was the logical first choice for the next earthquake of magnitude 8.0 or so on the Richter scale.

This time, however, nature confounds the scientists. They thought it unlikely that the next superquake would occur on the little Newport-Inglewood Fault Zone. But earthquakes are perhaps the least predictable of all natural phenomena, and this quake is no exception to that rule. Not only is its site unexpected, but its magnitude is a surprise as well. Little faults like this one commonly generate only moderate quakes, 6.0 or thereabouts. But on this occasion the Newport-Inglewood Fault Zone exceeds all expectations and delivers a 7.8 temblor, only a bit less powerful than the San Francisco earthquake of 1906. This quake will last seventy-five seconds altogether, counting a strong and almost immediate aftershock.

The focus of the quake is about eight miles deep. Its epicenter is midway between Venice and downtown Los Angeles. The S-waves and P-waves roll out from the quake's hypocenter in all directions, making half the state ring like a giant bell.

Geologists watching their instruments have seen these wave patterns before. The seismographs have told of other great earthquakes—in Mexico City, in Iran, in many far-flung parts of the world—but never before like this. This is the Big One, as Californians call it: the disaster California has been awaiting since 1906. These squiggles on paper are saying that a city is about to be destroyed, and thousands of persons in that city have only seconds to live.

For most of those caught in it, the earthquake begins with a low but rapidly growing rumble. The ground moves underfoot for forty-five seconds. After a brief pause, a thirty-second aftershock hits. There will be numerous aftershocks over the next few days, but none will add much to the damage caused by these first two quakes.

Suppose you could survey Los Angeles from a vantage point atop that skyscraper mentioned earlier. What would you see in the seventy-five seconds of the earthquake?

Don't worry about your own safety, for this building is capable of riding out the quake, thanks to modern materials and shrewd design. Though built of steel, the structure sways with the S-wave much like a resilient wood-frame home. The structure may lose a few windows and suffer other minor damage, but the building will stand. So take a good look at Los Angeles in the few terrifying seconds of the quake.

Downtown, the streets begin to undulate as the S-waves from the earthquake pass by. The quake could not have come at a worse time for motorists. This is the morning rush hour, and the potential for collisions is high even on an ordinary day.

When the asphalt under one's car is quivering like a gelatin dessert, it is impossible to drive a straight line. From your perch high above, the traffic appears to dissolve into chaos. Right-lane traffic veers left. Left-lane traffic swerves right. The result —head-on collisions as far as one can see.

About one in every five drivers veers off the road entirely and is stopped by obstacles on the pavement—lampposts, fire hydrants, bus kiosks—or by parked automobiles. The lucky motorists are wearing seat belts and shoulder harnesses and collide at relatively low velocities. Those drivers, though badly shaken, survive.

Motorists driving faster are less fortunate because of an inflexible law of physics having to do with moving objects. That law says the "kinetic energy" of a moving body (that is, the "punch" it packs if it hits something) increases not in proportion to its volocity, as one might think, but in proportion to the *square* of its velocity. This means a car moving at forty miles per hour has two squared, or four, times the kinetic energy of a car doing twenty.

When a car doing fifty or more collides with another car traveling in the opposite direction at the same speed, a terrific amount of kinetic energy gets released all at once. Not much can be done afterward except clean up the wreckage and pre- pare death certificates. That is exactly what happens on hundreds of streets all over greater Los Angeles when the quake strikes. After the rumble of the quake dies away, the first sound you are likely to hear is the squalling of horns from cars whose drivers are slumped, dead or unconscious, against the wheel.

Make a quick sweep of the cityscape with a pair of good binoculars, and you might surmise initially that little damage had occurred, except to luckless drivers. The city seems intact at first glance. No high-rise buildings have fallen. The famous Los Angeles skyline seems unchanged.

But a closer look reveals widespread damage. Where the sun strikes the pavement at just the right angle, you will see a glitter like that from spilled sugar crystals. The glints of light in this case come from shattered glass, thousands upon thousands of tons of it, scattered out into the streets where windows in homes, stores, and office buildings have broken under the force of the S-waves. Scattered amid the shards of glass is an avalanche of stone, brick, and mortar shaken loose from build- ing facades by the earthquake. About a thousand of those killed in this earthquake will eventually be ruled to have died of "pro- jectile wounds": the specialist's expression for veins and arteries slashed by flying glass and skulls crushed by falling chunks of stone.

Here and there around the city, faint puffs of smoke appear to be rising. They are not smoke from fires, though that will come later. These filmy clouds drifting upward are made of concrete dust and mark the points where buildings—mostly old structures built before the imposition of quake-resistant building codes—have collapsed.

In some cases a whole building has caved in, like a house of cards. Elsewhere the outer walls still stand, but the roof has given way and taken out all the floors below in its fall. And sometimes just the opposite occurs: the interior survives, but outer walls crumble like stale crackers into a cascade of debris. Anyone caught under such an avalanche will be lucky to live to tell about it.

Some buildings, especially those built during World War II and after, have come through the quake with surprisingly little damage. Here and there a structure stands practically untouched, windows unbroken, walls still vertical.

Yet only a few blocks away, other buildings are tilted at crazy angles. They appear to have sunk partly into the ground, like a brick dropped in wet cement. This is the work of liquefaction, the process by which passing S-waves transform unconsolidated material into a soupy mess that cannot support a building. As the S-waves passed, the sediments under portions of Los Angeles lost all cohesion. They could no longer hold the weight of even small buildings, and the structures built atop those sediments started listing like leaky ships. One small apartment building has rolled over on its side at an eighty-degree angle from the vertical, in a manner reminiscent of a St. Bernard stretching out for a nap. The building's tenants are evacuating the only way they can. They are climbing out the windows and walking down the now nearly horizontal wall, carrying their belongings in their arms.

The hills west of the city are difficult to see through the air pollution, but here and there a peculiarly light, parabolic patch of land is visible. Each of those patches represents a landslide. On the slopes, shear—the back-and-forth horizontal motion associated with earthquake vibrations—has overcome the internal cohesion of the soil, and hillsides have come tumbling down, carrying homes and highways with them. The gray-and-tan scars left behind have exposed the primeval rock of the mountains—the same rock that halted Baja California in its northward movement millions of years ago and in so doing created the geological conditions that have just destroyed much of Los Angeles.

When the casualty figures and damage estimates for the ninty-seven seconds of quake activity that day are tallied, the results are as follows:

- 42,000 persons killed
- $250 billion in property damage (not including subsequent fire and other earthquake-related causes)
- 125,000 injuries serious enough to require hospitalization
- 875,000 injuries not serious enough to require hospitalization

• Three major hospitals destroyed or so heavily damaged as to be unusable
• Water and electricity unavailable to 89 percent of greater Los Angeles residents
• 39 key communication facilities (satellite earth stations, Defense Department voice and data switches, and so on) destroyed or seriously damaged
• 90 percent of all major east-west roads and highways broken or blocked by landslides

These figures tell only part of the grim story; the initial damage is just a small portion of the loss caused by the earthquake. When all losses are considered—including such factors as increased unemployment, lower tax revenues, reduced productivity, and halted industrial output—the cost of this seventy-five-second vibration of the earth's crust will run far into the trillions of dollars.

If you have trouble imagining a trillion dollars, suppose you started today to spend $10 per second, $600 per minute, $36,000 per hour, $864,000 per day. You would reach the trillionth dollar in approximately the year 3400. To look at it another way: a trillion one-dollar bills, laid out side by side on the ground, would cover a square fifty-seven miles on a side. That is about the area of greater Los Angeles. And that is only $1 trillion. Multiply that figure by ten or fifteen, and you get enough dollar bills to cover New England. The next California superquake is liable to do that much damage.

Such figures are impressive, but they do not adequately convey the human element of an earthquake: the effect a quake has on people and their property. So let us look briefly at one hypothetical street in Los Angeles.

The street is two blocks long. Like much of the rest of Los Angeles, it is built on alluvium—unconsolidated material deposited by streams. The soil here is a fine-grained mixture of silt, clay, and sand. The U.S. Geological Survey would say it is moderately susceptible to liquefaction. It is not as resistant as the rocky soils of the San Gabriel Mountains to the east, but neither is it the kind of hazardous, soggy, fine-grained sediment one finds close to the ocean and in some other corners of the city where groundwater rises close to the surface. This street is about average, as liquefaction potential goes. In a superquake, however, even "moderate" liquefaction can look devastating by everyday standards, as we will see in a moment.

About half commercial and half residential, the street is dominated by a handsome five-story apartment building constructed in the twenties. Built of red sandstone with gray limestone trim, the structure shows surprisingly few signs of age, partly because of the warm, dry climate of southern California.

The apartment building is home to about thirty tenants, mostly young professionals. Their needs are served by approximately a dozen businesses on the street. There is a grocery, a service station, a sporting goods store, a hair salon, a print shop, and several other establishments. A block away is a small hospital, a four-story structure supported on concrete pillars, with parking on the ground level.

This morning a fuel truck is making a delivery to the service station on the corner. Thousands of gallons of gasoline are pouring through a hose from the truck's huge tank to the house-sized containers buried under the station. Teenagers enjoying the last few weeks of summer glide into and out of the sporting goods store on roller skates and roll up and down the sidewalks. Some skate into traffic, headphones on, lost in a blissful world of music. In the East drivers would slam on their brakes and swear at the skating teens, but in Los Angeles drivers are used to such minor perils and slow down to make sure the skaters come to no harm.

Skating is one way to keep cool on a hot day like this one. A less athletic approach is to sit at home beside a fan or air conditioner. As a result many persons are indoors at the moment of the quake and therefore at risk of being killed in collapsing buildings.

As the first shock hits, pedestrians and skaters alike lose their footing and fall on the pavement. The cement on which they stand is rippling like the water in a swimming pool as the S-waves sweep along the ground.

A split second later, plate-glass windows in stores on either side of the street shatter and fall outward onto the sidewalks in a cascade of razor-edged fragments. Awnings and overhangs come crashing down, trapping pedestrians underneath and killing some of them immediately. Halfway down the block a palm tree, its roots loosened by liquefaction, topples over slowly after being struck by an out-of-control automobile.

The driver of the automobile has, in effect, been killed thrice. His head has just made fatal contact with the windshield of his car; the steering column has speared his chest; and several packed suitcases in his trunk have smashed forward and struck him from behind with the force of rifle shells. His death is mercifully quick. He was killed before he knew what hit him. Not everyone will be so fortunate; all over the affected area, thousands of persons lie injured and buried in the debris of collapsed buildings. Some of those trapped individuals will be rescued quickly, but others will have to lie in pain for hours or even days before help arrives, and many will expire before rescuers can reach them.

In less than two minutes the quake has transformed the street into an awful caricature of its former appearance.

Palm trees lining the street are canted at strange angles. A couple of telephone poles are down. Roughly half the windows in sight are shattered, and several buildings look as if they had been melted out of shape like plastic toys in an oven. The front of the grocery remains mostly intact but is now canted back slightly from the street. That is because the rear portion of the building has collapsed. The roof has fallen, more or less in one piece, on the floor, with foodstuffs, shelving, and other assorted debris peeking out from in between. The result looks somewhat like a colossal, messy sandwich. The smells of spilled edibles waft out from under the debris: onions, tomatoes, vinegar, cheese, a hundred other aromas all mixed together with the chalky smell and taste of pulverized plaster and concrete dust in the air.

There is something else in the air, too: the smell of burning fuel. At the corner, a rising column of flame and black smoke reveals that the filling station has caught fire. It is easy to see what happened. The quake severed the hose being used to transfer fuel from the truck into the underground tanks, and generated some ignition source—perhaps a snapped light cable—that touched off the spilled gas. More gasoline is spilling every second because the driver fled and the station attendant, a boy in his teens, has no idea how to shut off the flow of flammable liquid. The pavement under the filling station has bulged upward slightly near the road where a half-empty tank, suddenly turned buoyant as the soil around it liquefied, has bobbed to the surface and pushed up the thin layer of concrete.

Displaced chunks of sidewalk litter the street. The earth-quake waves, in passing, lifted up sections of the concrete and scattered them like dominoes. The curb has separated from the pavement of the street, too; where once they were joined together, there is now a two- to three-inch gap. The street is fissured in dozens of places, and a foot-high ridge runs across the road where earlier the concrete was smooth. This ridge is a compressional feature, generated by the same forces that scattered the blocks of cement about the sidewalk.

A corner of the apartment building has collapsed, burying about a dozen tenants under the debris. The balconies have collapsed, too, but the stairwell is intact, and most of the building's surviving residents are able to make their way outside. Some of them are injured, but all are capable of walking, so those who need treatment set out for the nearby hospital. Their progress is slow because they will not recover their usual equilibrium for a few more minutes. The vibrations from the quake have affected the balance mechanisms in their inner ear, with much the same effect as a violent ride at a carnival. Right now they are staggering like drunks and pausing every minute or so for a look around.

Their cozy neighborhood has suddenly become a weird and unfamiliar place. The sporting goods store has lost its facade; the pavement in front is now covered with a heap of bricks and plaster. Miraculously, the hair salon is intact. Its windows are unbroken, and the sign above the door is still in place. But the print shop next to it is a total loss. The smell of ink from shattered bottles is heavy in the air around the shop's ruins. Whiffs of gas drift through the air, too, from ruptured mains.

A muffled explosion behind them makes the survivors turn around. Leaking gas has collected inside a store a block away and has been touched off by something inside. The blast knocks out the windows and blows open the front door, but the building stands. Curiously, there is no fire. The initial explosion consumes all the oxygen in the store, and in the depleted atmosphere left behind, further gas leaks cannot ignite.

At last the refugees arrive at the hospital. An ambulance is sitting, lights flashing, at the emergency entrance. Or rather, it sits where that entrance used to be. The emergency room was on the ground level of the hospital and was crushed when the eastern half of the building collapsed. The remainder could come down at any moment, for large fractures can be seen in the facade. Patients and nurses are looking out the windows in search of rescue but are effectively stranded, for stairwells at either end of the hospital have crumbled, cutting off all exits.

The hospital is a total loss. To make matters worse, it has been destroyed at the very moment when it is needed most. Injured men and women, the human wreckage from the quake, are starting to make their way there. Some can walk; others have to be carried. One woman arrives leaning on her husband's shoulder, a kitchen towel tied across her eyes. She is moaning, having apparently been blinded when the quake splashed some strong household chemical into her eyes. A boy about twelve years old is there, too, his right hand broken by a door that slammed shut on it during the first moments of the quake. Among those carried to the hospital—on a screen door since no stretcher was available—is a man in his twenties. His bearers set him down on the front lawn, but it soon becomes clear that the hospital will do him no good, for he is dead.

Scenes like these will be repeated in residential areas all over greater Los Angeles in the hours after the earthquake, because —as we saw earlier—many portions of the city and its suburbs are built on alluvium, which can make an already dangerous quake disastrous as the soil liquefies.

Some towns and neighborhoods weather the earthquake with relatively little damage, thanks to a combination of firm soil and quake-resistant architecture. But in other places the quake's effects are truly catastrophic. Portions of Lomita are devastated because much of that community is built on moist river-plain sediments. Former lake-bed sediments just to the north of Torrance liquify as well.

Generally speaking, the worst damage occurs along the ocean, where the liquefaction of wet, sandy, unconsolidated soil makes a ruin of settlements all along the coast from Malaga Cove, just north of Palos Verdes, to Santa Monica and beyond.

The shores of San Pedro Bay, site of Los Angeles Harbor and Long Beach Harbor, are perhaps the hardest hit. Here the soil grains lose all cohesion, and buildings tumble left and right.

Around Marina del Rey, a triangular area of some five square miles, running about three miles along the coast and five miles inland, is all but wiped out by liquefaction; the whole area appears to have been stirred by a giant, subterranean spoon. Houses lie canted at weird angles. Telephone poles and highway signs lean far off the vertical, as do some tall buildings. Highways lie fissured and twisted like broken skin on a pudding, while some parking lots are so thoroughly shattered that, when viewed from the air, they resemble alligator hide.

Here and there along the coast, one can see large circular openings in the ground, reminiscent of craters on the moon. Some of these holes are six feet wide or bigger, and all are surrounded by soggy deposits of sand. These formations are called *sand blows*. They occur where the rise in pore-water pressure forces groundwater and sediment up through the surface in a muddy, sandy geyser. In some places the fluid spurts twelve feet high and leaves yellow sand scattered in radial patterns around the hole, like the rays surrounding lunar craters.

But the sand blows and other effects of liquefaction are only part of the damage faced by people along the shores. This earthquake has also spawned a tsunami.

Offshore, the vibration from the Newport-Inglewood temblor has briefly activated the undersea fault zones. The submerged faults quiver for a few moments, releasing some of their pent-up energy: not much, but enough to cause turbidity flows—that is, submarine landslides—on the offshore slopes.

Large blocks of sediment shake loose from the seabed and start to slide downslope. As each slab of sediment breaks loose, it creates a depression at its upper end. The resulting suction makes water at the surface dip downward. This disturbance sends a small tsunami, about two feet high, rolling shoreward.

Another tsunami of about the same size originates when the slab comes to rest; its toe, or leading edge, bulges upward and causes a corresponding bulge on the surface, creating another seismic sea wave. This combination of processes occurs at several points offshore. The result: several tsunamis rippling toward Los Angeles.

None of these tsunamis individually would amount to much. But together they reinforce or cancel out one another in places, creating a complex pattern of waves. As they come ashore, the waves have devastating impact at some spots and almost no effect elsewhere.

At Long Beach, for example, the tsunami is unimpressive because the waves more or less nullify one another. The water level rises suddenly about a foot, then subsides. The process repeats itself several times before the waves exhaust themselves. Here the tsunami adds little or nothing to the destruction caused by the earthquake. The *Queen Mary* rides out the tsunamis, and even small craft in the harbor suffer little tsunami damage other than scraped paint and dented gunwales.

But elsewhere along the shore just the opposite occurs. Instead of canceling one another out, the tsunamis reinforce one another, creating large, destructive waves. In some places the ocean rises abruptly without warning, and a five-foot-high mass of water surges over the beaches, sweeping away anyone and anything in its path.

Other locations are given a brief warning before the tsunami strikes. The water retreats from the beach momentarily, with a loud hissing, sucking noise, exposing the sands on the bottom. Some people who are knowledgeable about tsunamis recognize the receding waters as a signal that a tsunami is on the way and make a hasty retreat to the highest local ground. Meanwhile the waters gather themselves up just offshore and return as a breaker capable of destroying homes, cars, or just about anything else. And this is not a single tsunami. Several others will follow, though they will add little to the destruction caused by the first.

Here we presume that an earthquake and submarine landslides are the only tsunamigenic agents involved. A large methane outburst from the seabed—a distinct possibility in view of the methane eruption that accompanied the 1971 San Fernando earthquake—could add still more power to the waves.

At this point readers may ask, Will Los Angeles fall into the sea when the next superquake strikes?

The answer is no. Though some alarmist articles and novels have contributed to the widespread fear that large portions of California will slip beneath the waves when the next big quake occurs, this worry is groundless.

As a rule very little vertical motion occurs in southern California quakes, except in a few spots such as the Hosgri Fault Zone offshore. Most crustal movements here are lateral—that is, side to side—rather than vertical, for reasons explained in chapter 2. So there is practically no chance that Los Angeles will tumble into the ocean. The popular image of California falling into the sea during an earthquake was probably inspired by accounts of tsunamis hitting the shore or by isolated coastal landslides.

Landslides will be a serious concern on land during the next superquake, partly because the hills around Los Angeles are thickly populated and partly because Los Angeles is served by several major highways that cut through the mountains to the east. Road cuts there are sure to suffer from landslides and rockfalls. Here is how one report on the effects of a hypothetical major quake in the L.A. area describes the anticipated damage to local highways:

> Interstate 5 from the San Joaquin Valley and Interstate 15 through Cajon Pass will be closed, leaving U.S. 101 along the coast as the only viable major route open from the north. Highway connections with San Diego will remain open. . . .
>
> In San Bernardino County, Interstate 15 will be closed by settlement of major fills and rockfalls in Cajon Canyon. Other freeway damage along Interstate 15E to the south, including major damage to the Interstate 15E/10 interchange, will result in closure of this route south to Riverside and Interstate 10 to the east.

It is impossible to overestimate the damage that a superquake will do to highways and to transportation in general in the L.A. area. We have seen already, in the previous chapter, what happened to the Los Angeles freeway system in the 1971 San Fernando earthquake—and that temblor was mild compared with the one that is expected to batter Los Angeles within the next few years.

Many of the city's major arteries will be knocked out for days, possibly weeks, after the next superquake; so will secondary roads that were shattered by the temblor and littered with fallen debris. Driving will be next to impossible in many areas of Los Angeles until the roads are cleared and repaired; and that transportation problem will prevent emergency vehicles, such as ambulances and fire trucks, from reaching many spots where they are needed.

Fire trucks especially will be required immediately following the quake if the temblor occurs in the dry season, as described here. Collapsing houses, falling power lines, and other situations will create countless point sources of ignition, so that blazes may break out all over the metropolitan area. Particularly at risk are homes in the hills outside the city, where grass and other vegetation tend to be so dry in summer that only the constant vigilance of homeowners and fire fighters prevents the area from burning up every year.

But following a superquake, fire fighters will be at a disadvantage, if not helpless. In some areas, at least, the quake is expected to shatter water mains and cut off the supply needed for dousing fires. And even if the water holds out, the roads are likely to be in such poor condition—cracked apart by the quake and choked with debris—that fire trucks will probably have trouble getting through.

Sprinkler systems and fireproof construction will help minimize fire damage in some areas, but even so, large areas of Los Angeles are bound to burn in the aftermath of the next superquake, just as happened to San Francisco in 1906. Moreover, the fires will be fed by thousands of concentrations of highly flammable liquids—a situation that did not exist in San Francisco early in this century. Fighting these blazes will be a tremendous task because many of them will be fueled by kerosene, gasoline, and other chemicals against which traditional firefighting methods (that is, water) are ineffective. As often as not, these fires will have to be left to burn themselves out. The resulting conflagration may last a week or longer.

Other dangerous chemicals are carried in huge amounts as cargo on Los Angeles roads. So all over the city, transportation accidents involving chemicals will probably add to the destruction caused by the earthquake itself. Indeed, chemical accidents are liable to be among the three leading causes of death and injury, along with fire and collapsing buildings.

Though we seldom stop to think about it, modern urban society is founded, to a large extent, on toxic chemicals. Chlorine, bromine, formaldehyde, benzene, cyanogen, nitrites, sulfites, ammonia—these and thousands more are carried into, and stored in, our cities in vast quantities. Some are used in pure form, for applications ranging from home heating to dry cleaning. Others are compounded with additional substances in the manufacture of millions of goods, from clothing to telephones.

But all these substances have one property in common: they are harmful to human life. For that reason they are ordinarily kept stored safely in special tanks or other containers. When those vessels are ruptured or upset by the earthquake, however, millions of pounds of dangerous chemicals will be released into the environment.

Consider, for example, what might happen if a tank car full of liquid chlorine were derailed on its way into the city. If some of the chlorine escaped, it would form a highly toxic cloud on contact with the air. Chlorine gas was considered an inhumane weapon when it was released on the battlefields of Europe during World War I, because when chlorine comes in contact with mucous membranes in the body, such as the lining of the respiratory system, it simply burns them away. Their lungs seared out, victims die almost immediately. This would be the likely fate of anyone caught in the cloud of gas escaping from that breached tank car.

Other poisons are carried on the highways in huge quantities. Imagine what might happen if a truck carrying a load of assorted insecticides toppled over on its side and released part of its toxic cargo. These are not mildly poisonous materials like the boric acid one sprinkles in dark corners to get rid of roaches. These spilled chemicals are among the most dangerous substances made outside the nuclear industry; and they are quick to vaporize in the summer heat. Soon a cloud of highly toxic vapor would start wafting outward from the site of the spill. Fortunately, the smell of the gas is unmistakable, and any reasonably alert person in the vicinity would be able to recognize it and run for safety.

The two scenarios you have just read are not mere speculation. They are based on actual incidents that have occurred in various parts of the United States in recent years. Safety standards for transportation of dangerous cargo in the United States are extremely lax, and even in the absence of natural disasters, serious accidents are commonplace. In 1986 Senator Albert Gore of Tennessee condemned U.S. regulation of hazardous-material shipments as "frighteningly inadequate," and at about the same time a report prepared by the Office of Technology Assessment (OTA) presented a terrifying picture of what can, and does, go wrong when dangerous cargoes are shipped around America.

OTA concluded that more than half of all hazardous-material spills are caused by human error, and that damage from such incidents is probably at least ten times greater than the annual total reported to Congress by the Transportation Department. Government regulation of shipments is handicapped, OTA pointed out, by poor coordination, shortages of funding and manpower, state and local regulations, inaccurate labeling of containers in shipments, and poor training for truck drivers and emergency officials. Federal inspection forces for carriers of hazardous materials were reduced by 50 percent between 1979 and 1984, the study said, while hazardous-material shipments by truck alone increase 3 to 4 percent annually. "In short," the report said, "the system is burdensome to industry without providing adequately for public health and safety." How a superquake will affect that system is unpleasant to consider.

Humankind is not the only species that will have its daily routines disrupted by the quake. Among the other denizens of our urban environment is the rat. Known to scientists as *Rattus norvegicus*, the Norway or brown rat infests greater Los Angeles by the millions. Some estimates put the city's rat population about equal to its human population, though the true proportion of rats to people may be much higher. The hardy but detested rat may become a serious threat to health in the days and weeks just after the superquake, partly because of the rat's high mobility.

Once it was believed that rats were homebodies. They were thought to set up small territories and stay there, feeding on whatever was at hand. Now that picture of rat society has changed greatly in light of recent research. Rather than lurking near home all the time, rats roam far afield on nightly forays in search of food. A given rat may travel a mile or more in a single trip and can run at astonishing speed. One rat fitted with a small radio transmitter was clocked at speeds exceeding those of human sprinters; the rat ran the length of a standard football field in slightly over ten seconds.

Now imagine hundreds of thousands of rats fleeing their dens at high speed in the moments before and during the earthquake. Some of those rats, in communities east of Los Angeles, find themselves cast out into the adjacent desert, where they come into contact with ground squirrels. These

little rodents are more endearing than rats but are also dangerous, for some of them are known to harbor the plague micro-
organism.

Though the word "plague" nowadays is generally applied to
any widespread and acute infectious illness, it refers specifically
to one disease, the malady that wiped out a third of Europe's
population in the Middle Ages. The plague occurs in two
forms: pneumonic plague affects the lungs, while bubonic
plague is characterized by large and painful swellings in the
"buboes," or groin. Both forms of plague are highly contagious
and can be fatal without prompt treatment.

Among the agents of the plague's spread is the flea. As the
rats roam among the ground squirrels, infected fleas hop onto
the rats and are carried back into the city when the rats retreat
from the less hospitable environment of the desert. Some of
the rats find their way into temporary tent cities set up in parks
and other open areas to house the homeless refugees from the
earthquake. At night rats in search of food come nosing
around the tents. Sometimes the fleas hop off the rats and onto
humans, but in other cases the transfer is less direct. A dog in
the camp catches a rat. Fleas leave the rat in favor of the dog
and make the leap from dog to human later, when the dog is
close to its owner. However fleas are transferred, they wind up
on humans, and their bites infect people with the plague mi-
crobe. A few days later the first cases of plague appear on the
outskirts of Los Angeles, and one of the scourges of ancient
times reappears in the modern world. Only prompt medical
attention and swift applications of rat poison avert a major
epidemic.

This is assuming, of course, that medical care is readily available for persons in those tent cities. That may not be the case.
Following a superquake, hospitals may have their hands full
trying to care for the injured and will be hard pressed to handle
even a fraction of the injuries caused by the earthquake; doctors will probably have to resort to the wartime practice of
triage, in which patients are separated into three categories:
those who will survive without prompt treatment, those who
can be saved with immediate care, and those who will die in any
event. Triage will force some difficult decisions from doctors
after the superquake.

For some time after the earthquake, Los Angeles may well

become a city under martial law. The National Guard and the army will almost certainly be required to help police maintain order and prevent looting. For an idea of what life in Los Angeles will be like then, reread the portion of chapter 1 dealing with General Funston's response to the 1906 San Francisco quake.

Though the quake will cause little physical destruction outside a fifty-mile radius from the epicenter, the temblor's other effects will ripple through the entire country. Insurance companies will be inundated with claims. Out-of-town firms with L.A. offices will have to do without those branches for a while; and if power failures caused by the quake wipe out vital commercial data in computer memories, companies may face losses in the billions of dollars. Thousands of eastern and midwestern firms that use parts manufactured in Los Angeles will have to find alternate sources or shut down indefinitely.

Government operations are likely to suffer, too. The U.S. space program, for example, relies heavily on hardware and software produced in Los Angeles and its environs. Many of those items are considered "criticality one," meaning a booster or spacecraft cannot fly without them. Consequently, in the weeks and months after a superquake in California, rockets and satellites may have to sit idle on the ground while the government scrounges for replacements. If a crucial military reconnaissance or communications satellite already in orbit fails during that time, and the United States is unable to replace it, the nation's military space system—on which our strategic defense largely depends—could suffer badly. Thus the shock from a California superquake could reach deep into space and all around the globe.

These are only a few of the expected effects of the coming California superquake. A whole shelf of books would be required to project them all. Morever, what you have just read may be an optimistic forecast. Under certain easy-to-imagine circumstances, the results of the quake could be far worse than described here.

Even more sobering is the thought that Los Angeles is only one of the areas of our country that are vulnerable to superquakes. As you are about to read, several major metropolitan areas may actually be in greater danger than southern California.

6

California Is Not Alone

estructive earthquakes in the United States are not confined to California. Major quakes have occurred over the last three hundred years in almost every corner of the country, from Maine to Malibu and from Amarillo to the Alberta border. Here are some of America's more quake-prone regions:

Alaska. The forty-ninth state has been the site of some of the most calamitous earthquakes of the twentieth century, because the southern coast of Alaska is a subduction zone, where the continental crust beneath Alaska collides with the oceanic crust under the Pacific Ocean. Among the results of this collision are earthquakes and volcanic eruptions. Most of the big quakes occur in southeast Alaska; the southwestern part of the state is relatively quake-free.

The most famous Alaskan earthquake is the Good Friday disaster of 1964. That quake was centered on the Denali Fault, which runs within a few miles of Anchorage and Valdez. At 5:26 A.M., the earth began to ripple. The shaking lasted less than a minute, but when it was over, much of Anchorage lay in ruins. Anchorage's main street was broken vertically into a string of cliffs, some of them more than ten feet high. Total damage to Anchorage amounted to more than $275 million.

The control tower at the airport was destroyed, and several residential neighborhoods were entirely lost to groundslides; the earth sagged like a falling soufflé and took whole streets and subdivisions with it.

More destructive than the earthquake itself was the tsunami that followed it. The wave spread outward from the epicenter of the quake at a speed exceeding two hundred miles per hour. It came ashore as a colossal breaker at communities all along the southern Alaska coast—Seward, Kodiak, Valdez—leaving death and destruction behind it. Much of southern Alaska's commercial fishing fleet was wiped out by the wave.

The Good Friday earthquake released about as much energy as the explosion of two hundred thousand one-megaton nuclear bombs, or some four thousand times more energy than the largest nuclear device ever exploded. The bomb that destroyed Hiroshima in 1945, by contrast, had a yield of about one-fiftieth of a megaton. So the Good Friday quake released roughly ten million times more energy than the Hiroshima bomb.

The 1964 earthquake was still a clear and painful memory for Alaskans when, in 1969, the Nixon administration began preparing to test a nuclear device underground on Amchitka Island, a tiny member of the Aleutians. Environmentalists were scared the explosion might set off a major earthquake accompanied by another catastrophic tsunami. Public opposition to the test was considerable. But it went ahead as planned, and no tsunami materialized, because Amchitka's corner of the Aleutian chain enjoys relative seismic stability. Tsunamis usually result from quakes farther to the east.

One Alaskan area of worry to geologists is the Yakataga seismic gap, on the southern Alaska shore about eighty miles east of Anchorage. A seismic gap is a stretch along an active earthquake zone where things have been quiet for a considerable number of years. If no major quakes have occurred in a gap for a couple of decades, geologists start to get suspicious, because the silence along the gap may indicate that stress is building up there, perhaps to the point of causing a major earthquake.

A spate of moderate quakes in the last few years suggests that the earth under this segment of Alaska's coast is starting to stir after a long slumber. A 1983 Geological Survey report tells why: "On July 12, 1983, a magnitude . . . 6.3 earthquake occurred about nineteen miles beneath the Columbia Glacier north of Prince William Sound. . . . The earthquake, which was felt throughout much of southern Alaska, was the largest [in the] . . . region since the great 1964 Alaska earthquake [of] magnitude 9.2. The Columbia Bay shock was one of a number of moderate-sized earthquakes that have occurred in recent months around the Yakataga seismic gap. . . . During the first nine months of 1983, more shocks of magnitude . . . 5.0 or larger have occurred within about one hundred miles of the gap than in any one-year interval since 1970 to 1971."

That is an ominous record. Geologists studying these quakes concluded that "one or more major earthquakes having magnitudes near 8.0 could occur anytime" in the Yakataga gap. There is no way of telling when such a quake may occur. The report cited earlier is careful to point out that "while there is a continuing potential for a major earthquake in the gap, there is no compelling evidence that the earthquake is substantially more likely to occur in the next several months than in the next decade or two."

Those are comforting words. On second reading, however, one realizes they say a superquake could strike southern Alaska twenty years from now—or next week. Whenever the earthquake does take place, the tsunami potential will probably be high. Remember that this same stretch of Alaskan coast generated the devastating tsunami on Good Friday in 1964.

South Carolina. The earthquake that hit Charleston on the evening of August 31, 1886, is generally considered the most destructive to occur on the Atlantic seaboard in historical times. It was felt over an area of almost three million square miles, from Canada to the Gulf of Mexico and from Bermuda westward into the Mississippi valley. Damage, however, was confined largely to Charleston. About a hundred buildings were destroyed, and nine-tenths of the remaining brick buildings were damaged.

Vibrations were strongest along a line running northeast to southwest between the towns of Woodstock and Rantowles, about twelve miles west of Charleston. Within that zone of maximum intensity, even resilient wood-frame homes were shaken down. Large fissures appeared in the soil, and from them "large quanitites of water and sand were ejected," reports one chronicler of the quake. One crater opened in the soil by the vibrations measured more than twenty feet wide.

The railroad running through Charleston was especially hard hit. Rails were twisted, ties split, and locomotives and cars derailed. The sandy, silty soil under Charleston was responsible for much of the demolition caused by the earthquake; much of the Carolina coast is underlain by poorly consolidated material that quivers like gelatin as S- and P-waves pass through it.

A century later scientists are still unsure just what caused the Charleston earthquake. No one geologic structure can be identified as the quake's source. But if it happened once, it can happen again. Most of the comparatively mild seismic activity in South Carolina since 1886 has been concentrated in the Charleston area.

The Pacific Northwest. Oregon and the state of Washington are well known for their volcanoes, but they are subject to strong quakes as well. Both phenomena are generated by the subduction of the Juan de Fuca crustal plate, the last surviving bit of a much larger plate that was destroyed by the westward advance of North America over the past fifty million years.

How big a threat from future quakes does the Pacific Northwest face? "A growing body of data suggests that a great earthquake . . . could occur in the Pacific Northwest," declared the U.S. Geological Survey in a 1983 report to Congress on earthquake hazards in the United States. By "great," the report meant a quake of magnitude 8.0 or higher on the Richter scale. That would make the earthquake comparable to the 1906 San Francisco catastrophe.

"In fiscal year 1983," the report continued, "two separate U.S.G.S.-university seismological teams completed a study of earthquake potential in the Pacific Northwest. They concluded that the northwestern United States may [represent] a major seismic gap which is locked and presently seismically quiet, but which may fail in great earthquakes in the future."

Superquakes in the Northwest could be even more destructive than in California, because of the pattern in which Oregon and Washington are settled. Eastern Washington and Oregon are largely high desert, so most of their population lives in a moist, fertile western corridor running from around Medford, Oregon, northward along the Willamette River valley through Portland, and from there to Seattle and its suburbs. Much of this area is underlain by river deposits and other poorly consolidated material that could liquefy in a major quake, with catastrophic results.

Hilly terrain along this corridor has also been settled, so there are places where homes cover hillsides as thickly as scales on a fish. Around Seattle, a hillside home or office with a view of Puget Sound is a status symbol, and the ambitious will go to great lengths to live and work in such prestigious sites. But how prestigious will they be following a strong earthquake? Many of their former occupants may find themselves sorting through the rubble of what had been their homes and offices.

The navy has a particular interest in the seismicity of Puget Sound, for that is the West Coast base for the giant Trident missile-firing submarines that provide much of America's sea-based nuclear deterrent. Subs and other navy vessels might encounter serious trouble if a powerful quake in the Puget Sound area damaged the Trident base severely or clogged the ship channel with rock and mud shaken loose from slopes along the water.

The U.S. Geological Survey admits that "although there is a paucity of present-day seismicity (as well as significant historical activity) in the shallow part of the subduction zone near the coast, moderate magnitude, deep-focus earthquakes apparently on the surface of the subducting plate occur near Puget Sound." This same pattern is observed in other subduction zones, where the descending plate does not begin to produce quake activity until it is well below the surface, some tens of miles from the subduction zone itself.

Look at a chart of quake activity in western Washington State for a decade or so, and you will see almost no dots indicating quake foci in the Pacific waters offshore. But activity picks up under the Olympic Peninsula, which separates the ocean from Puget Sound. On the chart, the sound itself is almost black with little dots marking the sources of small quakes (magnitude 2.0 to 3.0), and in about a dozen sites one sees the bigger circles that belong to moderate quakes, around 4.0. One of these moderate quakes jiggles Puget Sound every six months or so, on the average. Will the charts soon include a much larger circle, for a quake of 8.0 or greater? Only time will tell.

Utah. Though Utah is not widely known as a dangerous quake zone, earthquakes are common in and near the Wasatch

Mountains, and the quake potential there puts about nine-tenths of Utah's population at risk. This quake hazard worries the state government, and in recent years Utah has joined federal authorities in conducting several studies to see what might happen if a strong quake struck the state.

The results of those studies were startling. One U.S. Geological Survey study of potential dam failure reached the ironic conclusion that a big quake in Utah—one of the most arid states in the nation—could drown more people than it killed by other means. "The . . . potential risk to human life from the floods resulting from dam failure could far exceed the potential loss of life caused by the seismic event itself," the report concluded. "In fact, the potential loss of life related to dam failure is estimated to be an order of magnitude greater than those directly associated with an earthquake, or 23,000 versus 2,300, respectively."

Preparing for quakes and floods simultaneously is a formidable task, as a 1982 report from the State of Utah Multihazard Project reveals:

> The emergency room of an existing hospital, which was above the elevation of expected flooding, had previously been wanting when checked for seismic resistance. A planned addition to the hospital was modified to accommodate an emergency room in the seismically safe basement. Thus, it was assumed the public was assured an emergency medical treatment facility. However, while the initial treatment facility would survive floods as bad as any experienced in the area, it would not survive an earthquake, and on the other hand, while the new facility would survive an earthquake, it would not survive a flood. Just east of [Salt Lake] City, high in the Wasatch Mountains, are several large dams that probably would not survive a catastrophic earthquake. In [that] case, in about thirty minutes—the time it would take for floodwaters to reach the facility—the city would not have an earthquake-resistant emergency facility. . . .

New England. The northeastern states have been shaken repeatedly by strong quakes since the region was settled by Europeans. An earthquake in 1755, probably centered just off Cape Ann, damaged buildings all over eastern Massachusetts and knocked standing persons off their feet. B. A. Botkin, in his *Treasury of New England Folklore*, tells how this earthquake helped one Reverend Phillips, of Andover, Massachusetts, chastise his drowsy congregation. A few days before the quake, he had scolded his flock from the pulpit for "sleeping away a great part of the sermon." When the earthquake occurred the following Sunday, Phillips said he hoped the "glorious Lord of the Sabbath had given them such a shaking as would keep them awake through one sermon time." Several more strong earthquakes hit the Boston area in the following century, culminating one Sunday morning in an intense quake that caused panic in Boston's Back Bay neighborhood and sent thousands of Bostonians, some totally naked, running into the streets.

Earthquakes and their related phenomena have left their mark on the folklore of New England. Botkin cites three intriguing examples: the Moodus noises, the New Haven ghost ship, and the *Palatine* light.

The Moodus noises are mysterious sounds—like rifle shots, cannon fire, or thunder—that have long been heard in the vicinity of East Haddam, Connecticut, often in the company of earthquakes. Although one might think at first that someone named Moodus had given his name to the sounds, they in fact take their name from the Native American word for East Haddam: *Mackimoodus,* or "noisy place."

The natives had an explanation for the noises. They thought their god was angry at seeing the Englishmen's god moving into his territory and was growling a warning to the encroaching Europeans. The whites, on the other hand, saw the Native Americans as devil worshipers and suspected the Moodus noises might have something to do with satanic rituals said to be performed at powwows in the area.

One Reverend Hosmer took a skeptical view of the theory that demonic forces made the Moodus noises. Botkin quotes him as writing, in a 1729 letter to a friend in Boston: "Now whether there be anything diabolical in these things, I know not; but . . . sometimes we have heard them almost every day, and great numbers of them in the space of a year." Hosmer described the noises as "very dreadful" and resembling "slow thunder," or "cannon shot, or severe thunder, which shakes the houses."

Botkin quotes another East Haddam resident's account of the Moodus noises and accompanying ground movements:

> An earthquake was noticed on the 18th [of] May, 1791, about 10 o'clock P.M. It was perceived as far distant as Boston and New York. . . . Here, at that time, the concussion of the earth, and the roaring of the atmosphere, were most tremendous. Consternation and dread filled every house. . . . Since that time, the noises and shocks have been less frequent than before; though not a year passeth . . . but some of them are perceptible.

The Moodus noises became something of a tourist attraction in New England, and the locals learned to be patient with outsiders who came around hoping to hear mysterious booms and rumbles. (Those familiar with New England humor may appreciate the following story. East Haddam had a famous drum corps at one point, and it was sometimes hard to tell the Moodus noises from the din of the drummers. When visitors heard a sharp report and asked what it was, townspeople would reply, "Nothing but the drum corps boys.")

The tale of the New Haven ghost ship is one of New England's oldest and most colorful legends. There are several different versions of the story, but it goes roughly as follows. In the winter of 1646, a heavy-laden and unseaworthy merchantman set out from New Haven for London but was never seen again. The pious people of New Haven were anxious for news of their friends and colleagues on the vessel and prayed to God for some sign of the ship's fate.

One summer evening in 1647 about sunset, the story goes, a spectral sailing vessel appeared in the air above the harbor just as a thunderstorm was passing overhead. The ghost ship was visible for a few seconds, then appeared to capsize and sink, leaving only empty air behind. That vision was taken to be God's confirmation that the ship indeed had sunk.

The story of the New Haven ghost ship bears a strong likeness to the legend of the *Palatine* light. In 1752 or thereabouts, the ship *Palatine* is said to have set sail from Germany to New

England with a complement of wealthy passengers, business-men who saw great opportunities for profit in the New World. The ship never arrived. After six months it was written down as missing and presumed lost.

What happened to the ship and those on board will probably never be known. Possibly it sank in a storm or capsized from overloading. But rumors began circulating that foul play was involved in the ship's disappearance. The captain (it was said) had been murdered at sea by a mutinous crew, who then robbed and killed all their rich passengers, beached the *Palatine* somewhere, and set fire to it to destroy any evidence of their crimes.

Soon afterward it appeared that this gory rumor was con-firmed in a supernatural manner. Observers on the shores of Block Island Sound said they had witnessed the apparition of a fiery, spectral vessel hovering over the waters. Botkin quotes the Reverend S. T. Livermore, a nineteenth-century clergyman who made a special study of the *Palatine* light: "[The] legend is that she was somehow changed into a ship of fire, rising up from the waters of Block Island Sound . . . and gracefully sail-ing on this tack or that, mysteriously manned by an invisible captain and crew, until hull, spars, ropes, and sails all slowly vanished in the air or settled down into the deep. Nor was all of this a myth . . . for there is ample evidence that a very strange light once performed very strange freaks over these waters."

Probably the Reverend Livermore was right. People really were seeing something eerie offshore. The *Palatine* light was reported often by reputable witnesses, some of them on as many as a dozen occasions. The vision was always described as a fiery ship or some blazing entity just above the waters of the sound.

If the legends of the New Haven ghost ship and the *Palatine* light sound familiar, they should. We have seen already how methane outbursts from underground are associated with earthquake activity. In quake-prone New England, it seems reasonable to assume that large amounts of methane could erupt from the sea floor near the coastline; and if anything ignited a rich methane-air mixture just above the water's sur-face, the resulting fire would look very much like a spectral vessel. The surface of the sea holds enough static electricity on some occasions to touch off a methane fire in this manner, and there would surely have been plenty of electricity in the air on the evening the New Haven ghost ship was sighted, because a thunderstorm was passing by.

The shrewd Livermore guessed that something like a methane eruption must have been responsible for the mysterious apparitions off the coast. "Of this phenomenon no satisfactory explanation has ever been given," he wrote, but he suggested that the *Palatine* light might be "fed by gas rising through the water."

New England earthquakes can be frightening even when they do not inspire ghost stories. An earthquake in the autumn of 1983 shook Vermonters awake at six in the morning and was followed several minutes later by a sizable aftershock. The following week Burlingtonians could be seen wearing newly printed T-shirts with the legend "I survived the Vermont earthquake." No one was killed or injured, nor was there appreciable damage, but the psychological effects of the quake were considerable. One Vermonter told the author the following story:

> I was in bed when I felt the earthquake. At first I figured it was a bus or train passing nearby. Then I remembered my home was on a small side street where trucks didn't go, and the railroad tracks were almost ten miles away, in Essex Junction.
>
> Without stopping to think what I was doing, I got out of bed and stood in the doorway, because that's what I'm told you should do in an earthquake; that way you won't be injured if the ceiling falls. When the ceiling didn't fall after about sixty seconds, I let my breath out and went into the kitchen to fix breakfast. I didn't feel especially scared. In fact, I felt downright proud of myself. It was like being under fire and refusing to panic. In my imagination, I was awarding myself a medal for coolness in an earthquake, or something like that.
>
> Then the second quake hit. I felt the floor vibrate and looked down and saw the coffee oscillating and splashing in my cup. I felt a little less confident after that. It was as if the quake sensed my pride and was telling me, "Don't feel *too* secure."

What would happen if an earthquake of magnitude 8.0 or so —about as powerful as the 1906 San Francisco event—hit New England today? The effects would depend largely on where the quake occurred. The "stern and rockbound coast of Maine," as poets call it, would probably weather the quake with minimal damage, because many communities there are built right atop the ancient bedrock, so the soil beneath them would be unlikely to liquefy and make houses topple.

Southern New England, however, is another matter. Here large parts of the landscape, especially along the coast, are underlain by unconsolidated material, mostly sand and gravel left behind by retreating glaciers at the end of the last ice age. Moreover, parts of some coastal cities are mostly landfill. Boston's Back Bay is built on landfill trucked in from the hills just west of town in the mid-1800s. This whole area, approximately from Beacon Hill to Brighton, is built on geologically unstable material. It may seem solid enough as you walk down tree-lined Commonwealth Avenue from the Public Garden past the brown sandstone townhouses, in the shadows of Boston's skyscrapers; but in the event of a strong earthquake, much of the ground under this beautiful corner of Boston may turn to something with the consistency of oatmeal. What will happen then is unpleasant to think about.

Upstate New York and Quebec. Northern New York State is bordered by a high-intensity earthquake zone that runs along the St. Lawrence River valley between the United States and Canada, and reaches well into the Canadian province of Quebec. Mont Tremblant (Quaking Mountain), the popular wilderness vacation area in the Laurentides north of Montreal, is said to have been named for the vibrations caused by waterfalls in the area; but it seems much more likely that the mountain became known as "tremblant" following an earthquake.

The St. Lawrence River valley is a *rift*, a tensional feature created when two blocks of the earth's crust pull apart. Rifts are highly prone to earthquakes, and we will soon see how another area of rifting in North America has put much of the Midwest in danger from devastating earthquakes.

Mississippi River valley. Although California has been the site of the most destructive earthquakes thus far in this century, there is actually much greater potential for damage in the Mississippi River valley near St. Louis, Missouri. This area suffered the most powerful seismic disturbance in U.S. history during the winter of 1811–1812, when a series of tremendous earthquakes occurred near New Madrid, Missouri.

Catastrophic property damage and loss of life would have resulted if the New Madrid area had been densely populated in the early 1800s; fortunately the area was sparsely settled, and few lives were reported lost. Exactly how many were killed is impossible to say. Only eleven men, women, and children were formally reported lost on land (including six Native Americans who drowned when the riverbank on which they were sitting collapsed), but reports of overturned boats suggest the toll may have reached into the hundreds.

Most of the fatalities were caused by drowning when victims fell into the water. There is no record of anyone dying inside a collapsing building, partly because many residents of the New Madrid area wisely evacuated their homes and moved into temporary camps following the initial shock.

Native American legends reflected the unstable geology of the New Madrid area. The Chickasaw people, for example, told the story of how Reelfoot Lake in Louisiana was created. Chief Reelfoot, so named because he was clubfooted and walked with a peculiar lurching motion, abducted a bride from the Choctaw people, even though he had been warned in a dream that the earth would shake in fury if he carried the young woman away. As Reelfoot and his reluctant fiancée were about to be wed (the Chickasaws said), a mighty earthquake caused the ground to drop out from underfoot. The chief and the whole wedding party were drowned, and the river covered the site, forming Reelfoot Lake. This account may be accurate, for modern geologists have determined that Reelfoot Lake was indeed formed as a consequence of an earthquake in prehistoric times.

The New Madrid earthquakes of 1811–1812 were felt as far away as Washington, D.C., some one thousand miles distant, where the vibrations rattled windows and displaced crockery on shelves. Pedestrians in Richmond found it difficult to stand as the shock passed through Virginia, and in Kentucky the vibrations were so strong as to leave people feeling dizzy and disoriented.

A highly exaggerated account in the New York *Evening Post* told readers, "Here the earth [was] torn with furious convulsions, opened in huge trenches. . . . Everywhere nature itself seemed tottering on the verge of dissolution." The *Post* followed this account with a spurious report that Natchez, Mississippi, had been swallowed up by the earth, and four thousand persons had been killed. Natchez had only a fraction of that population in 1811.

A more factual report of one of the New Madrid earthquakes was printed in a New Orleans newspaper in January 1812:

> We have the following description of the earthquake from gentlemen who were on board a large barge . . . at anchor in the Mississippi a few leagues [a league was equal to about three miles] below New Madrid, on the night of the 13th of December. About two o'clock, all hands were awakened by the first shock; the impression was that the barge had dragged her anchor and was grounding on gravel. . . .
>
> At seven the next morning a second and very severe shock took place. The barge was under way—the river rose several feet; the trees on the shore shook; the banks in large columns tumbled in; hundreds of old trees that had lain perhaps a century at the bottom of the river appeared on the surface of the water; the feathered race [birds] took to the wing; the [sky] was covered with geese and ducks and various other . . . wild fowl; very little wind; the air was tainted with a nitrous and sulfurous smell. . . .

The shocks continued. Naturalist John James Audubon was badly frightened by one of them while riding his horse. Audubon wrote later that he noticed "a sudden and strange darkness rising from the western horizon" and took it to be merely an approaching thunderstorm. His horse, however, knew better. Audubon recalled:

> I had proceeded about a mile when I heard what I imagined to be the distant rumbling of a violent tornado. . . . All of a sudden [my horse] fell agroaning piteously, hung his head, and stood stock still, continuing to groan. . . . At that instant all the shrubs and trees began to move from their very roots, [and] the ground

rose and fell in successive furrows, like the ruffled waters of a lake.

The behavior of Audubon's horse was typical of animals in the vicinity. Both wild and domestic beasts were seen to act abnormally, even hysterically. One eyewitness to the New Madrid earthquakes reported seeing "bears, panthers, wolves, foxes . . . side by side with a number of wild deer, with their red tongues hanging out of their mouths." John Bradbury, a Scottish naturalist visiting the New Madrid area to collect botanical specimens, noticed that waterfowl settled in large numbers on boats, while on shore, small birds did the same to houses. Some birds even tried to alight on individual humans—"seeking the bosoms of men," as Bradbury put it.

The waterbirds had reason to be disturbed, for the river was behaving in a most atypical way. One observer wrote that "the current . . . was driven back upon its source [that is, reversed] with the greatest velocity for several hours, in consequence of an elevation of its bed."

A correspondent for the *Louisiana Gazette* related his experience of an earthquake in the December 21, 1811, issue:

> On Monday morning last, at a quarter past two . . . I was roused from sleep by the clamor of windows, doors, and furniture in tremulous motion, with a distant rumbling noise resembling a number of carriages passing over pavement. . . . In a few seconds the motion and subterraneous thunder increased more and more: believing the noise to proceed from north or northwest, and expecting the earth to be relieved by a volcanic eruption, I went out of doors and looked for the dreadful phenomenon. The agitation had now reached its utmost violence. I entered the house to snatch my family from its expected ruins, but before I could put my design in execution, the shock had ceased, having lasted about one and three-fourths minutes. The sky was obscured by a thick hazy fog, without a breath of air. . . .
>
> At forty-seven minutes past two, another shock was felt without any rumbling noise and [was] much less violent than the first; it lasted near two minutes.

Lesser shocks continued through the morning hours, until at 8:00 A.M. another strong earthquake shook the area. The *Gazette*'s correspondent noticed odd atmospheric phenomena this time:

> This was almost as violent as the first [shock]; accompanied with the usual noise, it lasted about half a minute. . . . The houses and fences appeared covered with a white frost, but on examination it was found to be vapor, not possessing the chilling cold of frost. . . . The moon was enshrouded in awful gloom. . . .
>
> On the margin of several of our rivers, pumice and other volcanic matter is found. . . . [Several] miles from this town, it is said that a volcano had ceased to burn for the last three years and is thought to have now broke [sic] out in some quarter of our country. . . .

As the earthquakes rolled on, they disrupted communications between the New Madrid area and the outside world. The *Gazette* complained on February 8, 1812: "On Thursday morning last, between two and three o'clock, we experienced the most severe shock of earthquake that we have yet felt; many houses are injured, and several chimneys thrown down; few hours pass without feeling slight vibrations of the earth. Should we ever obtain another mail, we shall be attentive in recording the progress in every quarter." On March 3, the *American Statesman*, Lexington, Kentucky, reported that "at Fort Pickering, the block house, which is almost a solid mass of hewn timber, trembled like an aspen leaf."

The New Madrid quakes are of special interest because the phenomenon of "earthquake light" was observed. Numerous eyewitnesses reported seeing bright flashes of light, or a dull glow, in the sky over a wide area. Some of these illuminations may have been lightning from thunderstorms; but James Lal Penick, in his excellent history of the New Madrid disturbances, points out that thunderstorms are rare in the deep South in December, and that in any case a very large mass of storms would have been required to account for all the reports received.

Were these mysterious glows and bursts of light produced by methane gas escaping from deep underground and catching fire from static electricity or other ignition sources at the surface, as the deep gas hypothesis mentioned in chapter 2 has it? Nothing in the historical record specifically contradicts that explanation. Perhaps future earthquakes will supply the evidence needed to link outgassing of methane with earthquake light.

Rumors of volcanoes following the New Madrid quakes were false. Volcanic activity ceased in Missouri millions of years ago. In the nineteenth century, however, the causes of earthquakes and volcanic activity were still poorly understood; and since the two phenomena are often linked, many observers naturally expected to find vulcanism wherever and whenever major quakes occurred. One journalistic hoaxster held eastern readers enthralled with his completely fictional account of a huge volcano arising in Missouri and roasting everything for miles around with vast outpourings of hot gas and molten rock. His ruse was soon uncovered, however, and the public had a good laugh at his expense.

No instruments were available in 1811 and 1812 to measure the intensity of the New Madrid earthquakes, but modern seismologists have reviewed the historical data and the geological evidence of the quakes (landslides, sand blows, and the like) and have concluded that the December 16, 1811, shock measured 8.5 on the Richter scale of earthquake magnitude, while the shocks on January 23 and February 7 of 1812 measured 8.4 and 8.8 respectively. These figures make the New Madrid earthquakes the most powerful in U.S. history.

Natural disasters are often accompanied by religious revivals, and the New Madrid quakes were no exceptions. Penick tells how a sulfurous smell that accompanied the earthquakes (possibly a venting of sulfur oxides or hydrogen sulfide gas from underground) convinced many midwesterners that Satan himself had something to do with the quake, or that God was releasing a touch of the underworld on New Madrid to scare the locals back into the fold. The result was a sudden wave of religious fervor. Itinerant preachers seized on the disaster as a way to bring conviction to errant sinners. One zealot named James Finley, at the moment a quake shook part of Kentucky, jumped onto a table and cried: "For the day of His wrath is come, and who shall be able to stand?" Not many, as it turned out; standing upright during a strong temblor took all one's strength and concentration. Apparently Finley had a field day scaring his listeners, for later he gloated over the "great terror" his audience had shown every time the earth resumed shaking.

Established churches gained a windfall from the earthquakes. Penick reports the Methodist churches in the affected area increased their membership by 50 percent between 1811 and 1812—more than fifty times the rate of growth for the Methodists in the United States as a whole. But not all these "earthquake Christians," as they were scornfully called, stayed converted. Backsliding resumed in earnest as soon as the memories of the dreadful shocks began to fade. Some skeptics went so far as to attribute the earthquake not to the wrath of God, but to a comet that had passed overhead just before the disaster. The ancient belief that comets cause catastrophes was still widespread in the early nineteenth century, and this same comet (Penick writes) appears to have been implicated by Leo Tolstoy in Napoleon's invasion of Russia, as told in Tolstoy's novel *War and Peace*.

The religious revival among the whites in the Mississippi River valley was accompanied by a similar phenomenon among the region's Native Americans. Indeed, the New Madrid earthquakes of 1811 and 1812 set in motion among the area's native peoples a chain of events that reached all the way to the White House and changed U.S. history dramatically.

Before the earthquakes, the tribes in the affected area had been dispirited and disorganized. They felt helpless in the face of the overwhelming power of the whites who were taking over their land. Disease and bad liquor (both of them imported, either deliberately or inadvertently, by the whites) also played a part in undermining the tribes' health and morale. But the quakes shook them out of their lethargy. Feeling the ground sway beneath them, they could hardly be blamed for concluding, as many whites did, that the maker of the world was sorely angry with the human race and could be placated only by drastic means.

The natives tried. At first their efforts took the form of public burnings. The frenzy of the Shawnees and Delawares was especially intense; they torched their own folk with abandon. This homicidal madness might have continued indefinitely, had not a charismatic leader—the great Shawnee chief Tecumseh—redirected the tribes' fear and violence into a social movement that changed U.S. history.

A gifted demagogue and master of tribal politics, Tecumseh was so renowned in his own time that it was not unknown for whites to name their children after him. (The most famous of his namesakes was the Union general William Tecumseh Sherman, who became notorious for his march through Georgia during the Civil War.) Tecumseh made his goal the unification of all tribes. Only unified resistance, he preached, could halt the invading whites.

Tecumseh was famed as a prophet and was said to have forecast—if not sent—the great earthquakes. On a visit to another chief's lodge at Tuckhabatchee, near the site of present-day Montgomery, Alabama, Tecumseh gave his talk on the need for intertribal unity. But his host seemed unconvinced, so Tecumseh added an eschatological flourish.

"You do not believe the Great Spirit has sent me," Tecumseh said. "You shall know. I leave Tuckhabatchee directly, and will go straight to Detroit. When I get there, I will stamp on the ground with my foot and shake down every house in Tuckhabatchee." Then Tecumseh departed.

As soon as Tecumseh arrived at Detroit, the story goes, Tuckhabatchee was destroyed by the New Madrid earthquakes. "Tecumseh has reached Detroit!" the people cried, and his reputation as a seer was secured.

Did Tecumseh really foresee the earthquakes, or was this tale merely manufactured to aid the great chief's cause? Probably the latter. Fantastic myths surround messiah figures, and Tecumseh was no exception. But his followers believed the tale and were convinced Tecumseh had the Great Spirit on his side.

For good measure, Tecumseh was aided in his crusade by his brother, Tenskwatawa, an influential mystic who had much the same galvanizing effect on his people that Savanarola had in Italy centuries before. While Tecumseh called for a secular alliance among the tribes, his brother preached the need for spiritual regeneration among the Native Americans. This alliance of religious rebirth and worldly politics worked well. It gave the tribes a cause to fight for, plus the moral strength that comes from believing one fights on the side of the angels.

Tecumseh's base of operations was a village on the Tippecanoe River in Indiana. From there he traveled all over the Midwest, trying to gather support for his cause. He was successful. Many tribes joined together under his leadership, and he even persuaded the British in Upper Canada (now Ontario) to aid his crusade with supplies and advisers.

This alliance between the British and the western tribes worried Washington. Tensions between the British and their former American colonies were running high and would soon escalate into the War of 1812. The United States knew it would have to break Tecumseh's confederacy before the great warrior could pose a serious military threat to America's northwest frontier.

So William Henry Harrison, the hard-drinking governor of the Indiana Territory, was sent to meet with Tecumseh and his brother, who was now known as "the Prophet." The meeting resolved nothing, and at dawn on November 7, 1811, at Tippecanoe Creek, Harrison and his army of eight hundred men suffered a surprise attack from Tecumseh's forces. Sixty-one Americans were killed and 127 wounded. An American counterattack drove back the native forces, however, and Harrison's men destroyed Tecumseh's settlement on the river. This skirmish went down in U.S. history as the Battle of Tippecanoe, and Harrison himself became known as "Tippecanoe" or "Old Tip." Tecumseh's troops faced Harrison's in battle again the following year, at the Thames River in Canada. Tecumseh was killed, and his British allies deserted him on the battlefield.

Thus ended the Native American rebellion that the New Madrid quakes had done so much to inspire and assist. Largely on the strength of his victory at Tippecanoe, the Whig party nominated Harrison for president in 1839. His running mate was John Tyler of Virginia. Their slogan, "Tippecanoe and Tyler, too," is perhaps the most famous in U.S. political history. The Democrats renominated then President Martin van Buren, an aristocrat with a reputation for high living. The 1840 election was no contest; Harrison, the war hero, carried nineteen of twenty-six states. He had only a few weeks to enjoy his triumph, however, for at his inauguration he caught a cold that developed rapidly into pneumonia, and he died exactly one month after taking the oath of office. The hero of Tippecanoe went to join Tecumseh, and the social and political aftermath of the New Madrid quakes died away—with one curious exception.

Though Tecumseh's crusade failed, the metaphysical side of

it survived as a continuing series of religious awakenings among Native Americans, culminating in "ghost dancing," a mystical ceremony that was an attempt to link the defeated native peoples with their imagined next world: a place where long-denied justice would prevail, whites would be punished for their crimes, and the sacred union between Native Americans and their land would be restored forever.

Ghost dancing was roughly equivalent to the hymn singing of the early Christians who prayed for deliverance from persecution and looked forward to Christ's return and the advent of the New Jerusalem. The ghost dancing ceremony was also perhaps the most peculiarly American form of worship, and it represented the last gasp of a social and historical movement that began with the New Madrid earthquakes of 1811 and 1812.

Though the New Madrid quakes left their mark on U.S. history and Native American religion, they were responsible for only a single small contribution to literature (if one can call this contribution literature). Its author was a New York glassmaker named Henry Schoolcraft, who had failed in business and moved west looking for a new start in life. He visited the New Madrid area several years after the earthquakes and was inspired to compose a ghastly epic poem telling how an imaginary King of the Metals grew angry at the westward movement of settlers from the East and used the earthquake to halt their progress.

The work was called *Transallegania, or the Groans of Missouri.* Its title is fitting, for groans are what his poem elicits from readers today. The following couplets are representative of the work:

> *The rivers they boiled like a pot over coals,*
> *And mortals fell prostrate, and prayed for their souls;*
> *Every rock on our borders cracked, quivered, and shrunk,*
> *And Nackitosh tumbled, and New Madrid sunk.*

Penick points out that "Nackitosh"—Schoolcraft's misspelling of Nachitoches, Mississippi—actually did not "tumble." He adds that Schoolcraft, who evidently was not encouraged to pursue a career as a poet, went on to become a leading authority on Native Americans.

The earth under Missouri and its adjacent states was relatively quiet for the next thirty years. Then the earthquake zone around New Madrid rumbled back to life in early 1843.

On January 4 or 5, the *Arkansas Star Gazette* in Little Rock reported, "a quaking of the earth was very sensibly felt here, attended by the rattling of windows, glasses, and cupboards, and the creaking of our wooden houses. . . . The shaking of the earth in this instance seemed to indicate a vibratory motion from northeast to southwest and continued for about the space of one minute."

In Memphis, "hundreds [ran] into the street," the *New Orleans Daily Picayune* reported, "in fear houses would tumble down. No damage done, unless it be to crockery ware. The vibrations of the earth lasted in all two minutes and were accompanied by a heavy rumbling sound." Several days later the *Picayune* added a few details: "The paroxysm commenced about twenty minutes before nine o'clock on the evening of the fourth instant, and lasted about half a minute, during which time . . . 'the firm-set earth did reel to and fro as a drunken man,' so violently indeed as to make hundreds run into the streets from fear that the houses they were in were about to tumble down. . . . There was quite a rush at the theater, and indeed everywhere else, to get out of doors, and the shrieks of females were heard in different quarters of the town." The paper compared the noise of the quake to "seventeen hundred and fifty heavy-loaded wagons . . . driving briskly along the street."

The quake "was preceded and accompanied with a rumbling sound, as of . . . thunder," the *Memphis Appeal* told its readers. "Opinions are various as to that period of duration—some supposing half a minute and some as much as two minutes—but all agree that it was a rather alarming affair and by far the severest since 1811. But little damage has been done to buildings. The coping of some chimneys has been removed, and we have heard of the prostration of a cotton shed."

A more colorful account was published in the *Memphis American Eagle:*

> At about half-past eight o'clock yesterday our city was visited by one of those awful throes of nature, so convulsive and terrible as to spread almost universal alarm

over the city. The firmest buildings trembled and cracked, and the earth reeled and rocked under a most terrific excitement. . . .

We were in our office at the moment, in the second story of a new block of brick buildings. The commencement of the jarring we [interpreted as] the violent undertaking of some person to shake open a door beneath us. But a moment afterward, the agitation seized the brick walls surrounding us, shaking and reeling them to such an extent as to knock down particles of brick and plaster, jarring the roof and whole building so as to impress us with the fear of the building's falling. . . .We hastily fled into the street for safety. . . . In the street was still a violent rocking of the earth, and a rattling and rumbling noise. . . . Cries and lamentations of many horror-stricken men and women were heard to fill the air.

The shock "lasted about two minutes," the *Eagle* went on, and reached its greatest intensity after about thirty seconds. Then it "gradually died away in a dismal rumbling sound." Numerous walls were "cracked and sunk," windows shattered, and a cotton shed was collapsed by the earthquake, the paper reported. "At our auction houses, which were filled with people, so alarming and precipitate was the rush into the street that many people were crushed and trampled upon by the affrighted crowd."

"The earthquake shook us considerably," wrote Mr. W. C. Love of St. Louis in a January 16 letter to his wife, who was in Indiana on the day of the quake. "I was on horseback, and supposed that my horse had started and stumbled."

The Mississippi River valley had no further trouble from quakes for the following half century. But in 1895 another powerful earthquake hit the area around Charleston, Missouri, just a few miles northeast of New Madrid. The shocks were strongest in a roughly banana-shaped area about one hundred miles long, running northeast to southwest with Cairo, Illinois, at its midpoint. The shock was felt as far away as West Virginia and northern Georgia.

The *St. Louis Post-Dispatch* of October 31 announced news of the earthquake with the following headlines:

AN EARTHQUAKE SHAKES THE CITY
Violent Seismic Disturbances Lasting Nearly a Minute
Felt Throughout the City
Houses Rocked, Windows Rattled,
and Brick Chimneys Toppled to the Ground

"A heavy shock of [an] earthquake was felt [in Memphis] this morning at 5:08," the *Post-Dispatch* reported. "The vibration was from east to west. Houses rocked, and people were almost spilled out of bed. The shock lasted about a minute and was preceded by a rumbling sound . . . [and] was felt all over town," the paper said. "Houses swayed to and fro, a number of chimneys fell, and several walls were cracked."

The news report continued:

> There were no casualties, and the damage to property consisted of the destruction of a few chimneys and . . . tottering walls. The German Lutheran Church, on Eighth and Walnut streets, got about the worst treatment. It will probably have to be torn down, as the walls are badly cracked.
>
> The shock or shocks, for there appear to have been two of them, were sufficiently violent . . . to arouse everyone who was asleep and to alarm those who were awake. There were panics in the hotels and the all-night resorts, and at the Western Union telegraph office the operators stampeded. . . .
>
> The first shock was a short and slight one. It was followed by a heavy rumbling . . . described by old soldiers as similar to the sound of artillery passing over a paved road. Then came a heavy trembling that endured for more than thirty seconds and did . . . damage to property. . . .
>
> Mrs. Anna Horrocks, living two doors from the [church] on Walnut, said . . . the shock was very sharp and severe, ringing the doorbell and creating the idea of burglars, murderers, and all kinds of awful things. She heard the cracking of the church walls distinctly.

Here are a few more quotes from Missourians caught in the 1895 quake:

"I got up with a club to look for the man under the bed."

"Every dog on earth seemed to be barking at once."

"The big show windows all cracked loudly, and I was so sure that some of them were broken that I lighted matches to examine them."

"A queer streak of light stretched over the sky just before the shock."

"Bells [at a hotel] began to ring with such violence that the dayboard is now out of order. Bells in the rooms wouldn't work well, and guests ran out [into] the halls in their night clothing to ring the hall bells."

"The shocks were choppy."

"A pyramid of tomato cans toppled over."

Another paper printed additional details of the quake: "Clocks were stopped, and windows rattled. . . . In the west end of the city, the people . . . rushed in alarm from their homes, and returned only after having become numb with cold. . . . The shock was the severest ever felt [in St. Louis] and lasted fully two minutes."

Another three-quarters of a century passed before the New Madrid Fault Zone gave midwesterners another scare. On November 9, 1968, a loud but relatively minor earthquake hit, knocking down chimneys on aged houses and dislodging plaster from walls and ceilings. Water splashed out of fish tanks, and articles shifted slightly on shelves. Overall, however, damage was slight.

The New Madrid earthquakes have long posed a puzzle for geologists, for the quakes would seem to violate the laws of plate tectonics. In Wegener's classical model, earthquake activity is concentrated along the edges of crustal plates. But Missouri is smack in the middle of the North American plate, more than a thousand miles from the junction of the North American and Pacific plates.

In theory, then, Missouri ought to be about as seismically active as a goldfish bowl. Yet the most powerful quakes in U.S. history struck here. Why?

The bedrock that holds the answer to the mystery is buried under thousands of feet of sediment. But with the help of seismological data and advanced techniques of computer analysis, geologists think they may have solved the riddle of the New Madrid quake zone.

To illustrate, let us take an imaginary trip back through time. Approximately two hundred million years ago, North America was still part of the supercontinent that Alfred Wegener called Pangaea. If you could look down on Pangaea from space, you would see a vast ovoid landmass stretching from pole to pole. Much of the land would look desolately gray and brown, for plant life was still largely confined to shorelines at this time, and the great grasslands and forests that cover vast stretches of our modern world had yet to appear.

Now imagine you could start moving quickly forward in time again, keeping an eye on Pangaea all the while. First you would see Pangaea split horizontally down the middle, like a dividing cell. The northern half, which Wegener called Laurussia, will become the continents of the Northern Hemisphere, while the southern half—Gondwanaland, in Wegener's terminology—will, generally speaking, give rise to the continents of the Southern Hemisphere.

Suddenly, North America breaks off from the western edge of Laurussia and starts sliding westward, impelled by the up-welling of molten rock along the midocean ridge. Water streams into the breach between North America and the rest of Laurussia.

Look closely at North America. Running north to south down the middle of the continent is what appears to be a tall, wide mountain range with its spine gouged out. It looks like a great scar with raised edges, sliced out of the heart of the continent. This is a rift valley. It is much like a midocean ridge, for it represents a spot where the crust is thin, and molten rock from the mantle is welling up to the surface.

Had the sea rolled into North America's heartland just then, that rift valley would itself have become a midocean ridge. And had the rift valley kept growing, it might have split North America in half, just as the midocean ridge in what is now the Atlantic Ocean pushed North America and Laurussia apart earlier.

But something happened to the rift valley in North America's interior. It cooled off and died. As it cooled, the rocks at the surface "deflated," so to speak, and the crustal rocks dropped, creating a deep, wide valley with towering walls. This grand collapse generated great cracks—fault lines—in North America's midsection. In effect, these faults divide the eastern

United States from the western states. Over millions of years the faults were buried under deep layers of sediment, so they are not clearly visible today, as the San Andreas Fault is in California.

Yet the midwestern faults are as active as the San Andreas. They are not dead merely because they lie in the middle of the continent. Instead they remain active because of sea-floor spreading along the mid-Atlantic ridge, some four thousand miles away.

How can such a distant phenomenon generate earthquakes in America's heartland? Remember that new crust is forming all the time along the mid-Atlantic ridge. As the freshly solidified crust moves westward, on the U.S. side of the Atlantic, the new crust exerts a push on the eastern half of North America. This push, in turn, makes the eastern United States grind against the western half of the country, on the other side of those great buried faults along the Mississippi River valley. The result: earthquakes, some of them powerful enough to be felt more than a thousand miles away.

But here is another puzzle. The San Francisco earthquake of 1906 was roughly comparable in magnitude to the New Madrid quakes of 1811–1812, yet the San Francisco event did not shake half a continent, as the New Madrid quakes did. What carried the shock from the Mississippi River valley over such a vast area?

The answer has to do with the rocks far underground. Remember we noted how the character of bedrock can affect transmission of earthquake waves. If the bedrock is broken up, crumpled, and fractured by geological pressures, then the broken rock acts as a shock absorber and makes the waves die out in a relatively short space. "It's a little like tossing a baseball at a feather pillow," says one geologist. "The effects of the shock are localized."

This is what happens in California. The rock strata underlying the Golden State have been so cracked and jumbled together by the collision of North America with the Pacific crustal plate that they form a barrier of sorts to quake vibrations. Consequently the shock from the San Francisco quake of 1906 was not felt farther east than the Rockies.

In the eastern United States, however, the picture is much different—and potentially more dangerous. The rocks under

BIG WAVES   SMALLER WAVES   LITTLE WAVES

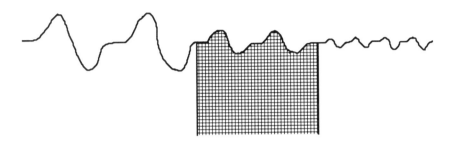

Damping Effect: Some materials act as earthquake "dampers," absorbing the energy of earthquake waves and localizing their effects. Here a zone of highly fractured rock (shaded area) is shown damping waves approaching from the left. *(Courtesy of Allan Frank)*

the Midwest and East are much more continuous than those beneath California. In the East, it is nothing unusual to be able to trace a certain rock formation for hundreds of miles in an east-west direction. This difference in subsurface geology has serious implications for the East if and when another major quake strikes in the New Madrid area, for these relatively unbroken formations underground could act as long-distance conduits for quake vibrations.

To return to our baseball simile, a superquake in the Mississippi River valley would be like tossing the ball at a Chinese gong instead of a pillow. Half the country would resonate under the force of the earthquake because the unbroken rocks below ground would carry the vibrations a thousand miles or more. The impact of the shock would diminish with distance; but even so, a powerful quake in the Midwest could cause alarm, if not substantial damage, over perhaps a million square miles of the continental United States.

What exactly could the United States expect from a repeat of the New Madrid quakes of almost two hundred years ago?

The U.S. Geological Survey has performed a computer analysis of the effects of such an earthquake, and the findings of that study are eye-opening.

Let us suppose, as the U.S. Geological Survey did, that an earthquake of Richter magnitude 8.6—about equal to the 1811–1812 quakes—strikes tomorrow in the New Madrid seismic zone. The quake would hit hardest along a stretch of the Mississippi River valley roughly 150 miles long, running from the Tennessee-Mississippi state line in the south to a point just north of where Tennessee, Kentucky, and Missouri meet.

But the quake would be felt far beyond this little corner of the valley. Here is how several major U.S. cities would experience the quake:

- *Chicago, Illinois.* Downtown skyscrapers sway back and forth, and passengers on trains can feel the vibrations transferred through the rails. Pedestrians are alarmed to feel the pavement vibrate underfoot, and they can hear tree branches rattle and rustle as the limbs swing in time to the S-waves. Church bells ring on their own. Plaster falls from ceilings in older buildings, while books in the public library are knocked off shelves. At City Hall heavy file cabinets are moved half an inch in the direction of the vibrations. Bars and restaurants lose substantial amounts of tableware as glasses, cups, and plates are shaken off counters and shelves. No one is killed, however, and no injuries are reported.
- *Carbondale, Illinois.* This quiet college town, home to Southern Illinois University, is much closer to the focus of the quake and therefore harder hit than Chicago. Here a general panic occurs. The noise of the quake is loud, and people run out of buildings in a state of near hysteria as buildings tremble under the force of the earthquake. Damage even to new, well-constructed buildings is considerable. Several stores and about fifty houses are destroyed. Casualties number in the hundreds because of collapsing buildings, falling plaster, overturned heavy furniture, and automobiles sent out of control by the shock.
- *Evansville, Indiana.* Evansville fares slightly better than Carbondale. The population is frightened, plaster falls in large amounts all over the city, and windows shatter in nu-

merous buildings, but casualties are few. Property damage is extensive in the southern part of town near the Ohio River, however, and the river itself is agitated by the earthquake. The U.S. Geological Survey notes that "a strong earthquake probably would not cause landslides throughout most of the city; however, landslides probably would occur along the steeper bluffs adjacent to the Ohio River." Liquefaction would most likely be confined to the river-deposited flood plain sediments.

• *Little Rock, Arkansas.* About a fourth of the city—mostly in North Little Rock, between the Arkansas River and Interstate 40—gets a heavy shaking from the earthquake, but only two townspeople are killed, and serious injuries are rare. Property damage in the rest of Little Rock is light. There is some liquefaction, but mostly on the floodplain deposits near the river.

• *Akron, Ohio.* More than five hundred miles from the focus of the earthquake, Akron is badly shaken. No one is killed or badly injured, but light damage to homes and businesses is widespread, and several old buildings are fractured so badly that they have to be condemned.

• *Atlanta, Georgia.* Office workers in downtown skyscrapers feel the quake plainly as their buildings start swaying.

• *Cambridge, Massachusetts.* The shock can be felt on the upper floors of the earth and planetary sciences building at the Massachusetts Institute of Technology.

• *McKeesport, Pennsylvania.* A painter on a scaffold is knocked off balance by vibrations from the quake and falls. Fortunately he is wearing a safety strap and escapes injury.

• *Washington, D.C.* Visitors to the Washington Monument feel a vibration but attribute it to the noise from a jet landing at nearby National Airport.

• *Memphis, Tennessee.* Memphis feels the earthquake severely, for it lies right on the edge of the New Madrid quake zone. Roughly half the city, in an area stretching southwest to northeast along the Mississippi and Loosahatchie rivers, is convulsed by fierce ground motion. Even the less severely affected parts of town suffer worse from the quake than Carbondale did.

Wood-frame houses and masonry structures built specifically to withstand earthquakes are thrown off their foundations, while less resistant structures are shaken down entirely. Large cracks open in the ground. Chimneys and monuments topple. The Mississippi splashes over its banks in waves taller than a man. Virtually every windowpane in town is broken, and pedestrians are knocked off their feet.

The earthquake disrupts vehicular traffic totally and causes hundreds of collisions and other accidents. In several parts of town, notably along Interstate 55 near the river, liquefaction sends buildings tumbling like a child's toys. About two square miles of downtown Memphis, roughly between Route 23 and the Wolf River, also suffer serious damage from liquefaction. Bluffs along the Mississippi crumble and fall into the water, while large blocks of earth one hundred to two hundred feet back from the river, their underpinnings liquefied by the earthquake, slide ponderously toward the water.

• *St. Louis, Missouri.* This is probably where the blow will hit hardest. A densely settled urban area built mostly atop geologically unstable sediment (much of it loess, a loamy, wind-deposited soil) with groundwater rising close to the surface, St. Louis is a case study in high liquefaction potential. These deposits are deep, many of them exceeding one hundred feet; and when the S-waves from the earthquake pass through, they will turn into something resembling a titanic mud pie. The U.S. Geological Survey predicts what will happen then:

> Much of the old part of the city of St. Louis, and particularly the modern highway network, is built on uncontrolled fill. This fill is generally [found] in stream valleys, but there are many rubbish-filled pits in the old portion of the city. All this rubbish and fill is prone to large differential settlements in an earthquake.

"Large differential settlements" is how a geologist would describe a chaotic collapse of much of the downtown area. "In addition," the report adds, "parts of the downtown area are underlain by open, underground mines, where clay was long ago mined for making tile. Their locations are generally . . . not known." Already the ground is starting to sag over some of these mine sites. Undoubtedly many more of them will make their whereabouts known in the event of a superquake.

Landslides are another peril, as the U.S. Geological Survey report points out:

> Landslides [in the St. Louis region] are likely to be commonplace on many natural and highway . . . slopes. The natural slopes most prone to landslides in uplands are thick, silt-rich loess on steep slopes. . . . Many highway [cuts] will fail and cause very serious problems to highway traffic. Even today, there are significant landslides in the . . . cuts along I-44, I-244, I-270, and U.S. 67. Some highway fills [that is, the material in the roadbed underlying the asphalt] would probably fail, especially those on the lake sediments near the airport and on flood plains of the major rivers.

In other words, motorists on interstate highways cut through the hills around St. Louis are likely to find themselves slipping and sliding in all directions as the roadbed beneath them loses cohesion. And if they are spared that nightmare, the drivers may well get bombarded from above by landslides on road cuts.

In any future earthquake, the Midwest and South face an additional danger from *karst topography*. Better known as "sinkhole country," karst topography is characterized by large underground cavities dissolved in limestone rock by subterranean water. From time to time a cavity will collapse, creating a sinkhole that swallows up whatever sits atop it. Sinkholes in the southern and midwestern limestone country have been known to engulf automobiles and even entire homes. Until they give way, sinkholes are not always easy to detect, and engineers tell horror stories about office buildings and hospitals being built unwittingly on top of sinkholes, which then had to be filled by pumping gravel and concrete into them.

The weight of a passing car can make a sinkhole collapse. It is much more likely, then, that an earthquake may create gaping holes in the ground. Whenever the next superquake strikes the New Madrid seismic zone, midwesterners may find themselves crawling out of house- and car-sized sinkholes.

A superquake in the Mississippi River valley is likely to create an especially sinister environmental hazard that did not exist when the great earthquakes struck in 1811 and 1812. Since then the valley has become home to a vast chemical industry dealing in thousands of chemicals that are dangerous or even fatal to humans. These include the following:

- *Aldrin.* A gram (one-fifth the weight of a nickel) of this insecticide can kill several hundred birds.
- *Endrin.* An insecticide closely related to aldrin, endrin is an estimated three hundred times more poisonous than DDT.
- *Dioxin.* A widely used pesticide, dioxin is seventy thousand times more toxic than cyanide. Dioxin is lethal in extremely small amounts. A grain of dioxin almost too small for a person to see with the unaided eye can kill a guinea pig.
- *Methyl isothiocyanate.* This poison is very similar to the one that was responsible for the recent chemical plant disaster in Bhopal, India.
- *Tolune.* This paint thinner and varnish ingredient can impair the function of the brain.
- *Trichlorobenzene.* A dry-cleaning fluid, it can cause skin inflammation, kidney damage, and irregular heartbeat.
- *Chloroform.* It is a known carcinogen, or cancer-causing agent.

In a geologically stable area, this situation would be frightening. But in the Midwest, vulnerable as it is to powerful earthquakes, the potential for a devastating chemical accident in some future quake is almost too horrible to consider.

Let us consider it nonetheless. Suppose a quake roughly equal in magnitude to the initial shock of the 1811–1812 New Madrid earthquakes hit that area again today. Among the areas most strongly shaken would be Memphis; and whatever damage the temblor did to buildings there, the harm from chemical spills could be hundreds of times worse. A 1980 report released by the Environmental Protection Agency (EPA) estimated that there were probably more than one hundred sites in Memphis alone where hazardous wastes were buried or stored. Some are in landfills. Other quantities of hazardous chemicals may be hidden in slag heaps, at factories, practically anywhere. Numerous toxic chemicals are manufactured in Memphis—so many, in fact, that chlorinated hydrocarbons have been found in high concentrations in the Wolf and Loosahatchie rivers, and fishing has been outlawed for about thirty miles downriver from Memphis because of high levels of toxic materials in the waters. It takes very little imagination to conceive of what may happen to Memphis if even a small fraction of such chemicals, whether stored or in the process of manufacture, were spilled by a superquake.

The Mississippi River itself could spread environmental poisons over wide areas of land during a powerful earthquake. So polluted is the Mississippi that at some locations in Louisiana water samples have been analyzed and found to contain approximately 750,000 parts per million of chlorinated hydrocarbons. In other words, roughly three-fourths of the river was pure liquid poison.

Not every stretch of the Mississippi approaches that toxicity, but some parts of it—notably near the New Madrid quake zone —are so badly polluted that fishing in them is officially discouraged. If the river happened to overflow its banks during a future superquake, midwesterners might find themselves not fishing but swimming in it as the waters spilled onto dry land under the force of the earthquake. Remember how eyewitnesses described the river's convulsions during the earthquakes almost two hundred years ago. If the river slopped over its banks during those earthquakes, it might do so again in any forthcoming temblor.

Now imagine swimming in a toxic waste disposal area. That, in a sense, is just what residents of the New Madrid quake zone may find themselves doing someday, because a hazardous waste dump is exactly what the Mississippi has become.

There is another potential source of toxins to consider here, too: sediments at the river bottom. The silt and mud at the bottom of the Mississippi and its tributaries have been accumulating toxic chemicals for years, and part of that chemical load is liable to be released if S-waves from a strong earthquake upset the Memphis–St. Louis region anytime soon.

The 1811–1812 earthquakes were disruptive enough to free ancient tree trunks from the grip of mud and silt on the riverbed and send the trees bobbing to the surface. If that quake could liberate the sunken trees, a quake of comparable magnitude today could reasonably be expected to release huge amounts of buried toxic chemicals from their resting places on the Mississippi bottom and send them drifting downstream as a wave of poison, all the way to the Gulf of Mexico—the body of water that provides much of the seafood on which the peoples of North America dine. The consequences for marine ecology in the Gulf of Mexico, and for the health of humans who consume its seafood, could be staggering.

America's earthquake hazards, in summary, are not confined to California. Indeed, Californians may enjoy the best protection against earthquakes because of their long and painfully educational experience with mightly temblors. The rest of the United States needs to realize that destructive quakes may strike almost anywhere, at any time, from coast to coast and border to border.

There are two lines of defense against earthquakes: prediction and preparation. Let us look finally at the prospects for quake prediction and what we as individuals and communities can do to minimize the effects of any major tremors that may strike.

7

The Problem of Prediction

When?

That question is much on the minds of Californians whenever they talk about the coming superquake. Indeed, earthquake prediction has been a topic of intense interest for centuries. Long before the prophet Cricksor issued his ill-fated earthquake forecasts, "earthquake prophets" were making headlines. One such charlatan created widespread panic during the reign of Henry VIII in England by pretending to forecast a major earthquake, and other quacks in succeeding centuries achieved similar results with bogus prophecies. Charles Mackay, in his 1841 history *Extraordinary Popular Delusions and the Madness of Crowds*, tells of one eighteenth-century seer who terrified Britain with a quake prediction:

> In the year 1761, the citizens of London were alarmed by two shocks of an earthquake, and the prophecy of a third which [supposedly] was to destroy them altogether. The first shock was felt on the eighth of February and threw down several chimneys in the neighborhood of Limehouse and Poplar; the second happened on the eighth of March and was chiefly felt

in the north of London. . . . It soon became the subject of general remark, that there was an interval of exactly a month between the shocks; and a crack-brained fellow named Bell, a soldier in the Life Guards, was so impressed with the idea that there would be a third in another month that he lost his senses altogether and ran about the streets predicting the destruction of London on the fifth of April.

Why Bell chose April 5 instead of April 8—an exact month after the second quake—Mackay does not say. Mackay does point out, however, that "most people thought that the *first* [that is, April Fools] would have been a more appropriate day." Next, Mackay tells how the public received Bell's prediction:

There were not wanting thousands who confidently believed the prediction and took measures to transport themselves and their families from the scene of the impending calamity. As the awful day approached, the excitement became intense, and great numbers of credulous people [migrated] to all the villages within . . . twenty miles, awaiting the doom of London. Islington, Highgate, Hampstead, Harrow, and Blackheath were crowded with panic-stricken fugitives who paid exorbitant prices for accommodation to the housekeepers of these secure retreats. Such as could not affort to pay for lodgings at any of these places remained in London until two or three days before the time [of the prediction], then encamped in the surrounding fields, awaiting the tremendous shock which was to lay their high city all level with the dust.

As the day of London's predicted doom approached, even skeptics decided it might not hurt to take a few precautions:

[The] fear became contagious, and hundreds who had laughed at the prediction a week before packed up their goods when they saw others doing so and hastened away. The [Thames] river was thought to be a place of great security, and all the merchant vessels in the port were filled with people who passed the night between the fourth and fifth on board, expecting every instant to see St. Paul's totter and the towers of Westminster Abbey rock . . . and fall amid a cloud of dust.

Of course, the great earthquake never occurred. London remained standing at the end of April 5, and many Londoners who had put their faith in Bell felt acutely embarrassed. "The greater part of the fugitives returned on the following day," Mackay writes, "convinced that the prophet was a false one; but many judged it more prudent to allow a week to elapse before they trusted their dear limbs in London."

Bell's career as a seer was over. He "lost all credit in a short time," Mackay reports, "and was looked on even by the most credulous as a mere madman. He tried some other prophecies, but nobody was deceived by them; and . . . a few months afterwards, he was confined in a lunatic asylum."

Bell may have been a little less angry than he sounded. He apparently was using a primitive mathematical model—that is, a one-month interval between shocks—to predict the date of the next earthquake. Today scientists are using centuries' worth of earthquake data to devise more sophisticated models of earthquake activity, in hopes of forecasting the date of the next California superquake.

Yet no reliable and exact forecast is available. Geologists are reasonably sure that a superquake is due to hit southern California within the next half century, but for now it is impossible to be more precise than that, because modern seismology is still an infant science.

Less than two decades ago the picture looked much brighter for quake prediction. Hopes were high then that scientists could soon devise a way of predicting highly destructive earthquakes. Around 1970 one prominent Soviet geologist was widely quoted as saying a workable system of quake prediction would be invented "within the next ten years."

It was not. Geologists have had some success predicting small earthquakes, such as those that jiggle the boundary region between upstate New York and Quebec, but the big ones, the city busters like the 1971 San Fernando disaster or the earthquake that destroyed much of Mexico City in 1985, have foiled all efforts at prediction.

Time, place, magnitude: those are the three parameters that

a successful earthquake prediction must specify to a fair degree of accuracy. As a rule the latter two are much easier to establish than the first. We know that a superquake is due to strike southern California in the not-too-distant future, but figuring the date of the quake is next to impossible.

One big problem is the lack of historical data for southern California. Major earthquakes are not everyday events, even in such a quake-prone region. Besides, the entire historical record of California earthquakes, large and small, extends back only a little over two hundred years. With a longer record to draw on —say, something approaching the three-thousand-year-old base of earthquake data that one finds in China—geologists would be better equipped to seek out cyclical patterns in California earthquakes. Once a regular cycle is uncovered, scientists can say with some certainty when another major earthquake is expected.

But seismology is not expected to reach that degree of sophistication and reliability for many years to come. And if and when it does, will quake predictions really be desirable?

That may seem an absurd question. Yet history has shown that quake predictions, even absurd ones such as Bell's and Cricksor's, may prove almost as devastating as an actual earthquake. Cricksor's phony forecast, remember, had grave effects on property values in San Francisco and caused widespread social dislocation as the fearful fled the city. Bell's "prophecy," as we just saw, disrupted London so badly that the consequent loss of productivity probably ran well into the millions of dollars—as much economic damage as a moderate earthquake would have caused.

Another potential hazard in earthquake prediction is that it could lull the public into a false sense of security. Dr. Charles Richter once expressed misgivings over quake prediction research on the ground that it tended to divert public attention from the need to prepare for earthquakes. One may not be able to predict and avoid earthquakes, he pointed out, but one can do much to get ready for them, and survive them, whenever they may occur.

Californians, more than perhaps anyone else in the United States, have taken Richter's commonsense advice to heart. Whenever the next superquake happens, Californians intend to be prepared for it. Among the groups trying to get ready for the next major earthquake is the Southern California Earthquake Preparedness Project (SCEPP), a joint effort among state, local, and federal agencies to identify areas and situations of high risk and correct their weaknesses for the next superquake. In recent years, for example, SCEPP has

- Developed prototype quake response plans for a county, a small to medium-sized city, and a high-rise office building
- Formulated strategies and materials for public relations campaigns
- Developed a prediction response plan for Los Angeles
- Drawn up guidelines to help small businesses prepare for earthquakes
- Devised preparedness information for persons with disabilities
- Compiled research information on legal liabilities, disaster assistance capabilities, and insurance availability

On the individual and family level, there is much that one can do to be prepared for a future earthquake. The following measures are excerpted from U.S Geological Survey literature.

How to Protect Yourself in an Earthquake

If you live in an earthquake-prone part of the country, you may wish to prepare for quakes. A few commonsense precautions will reduce your chance of injury and might even save your life.

- Stay calm. Panic is likely to cause you much more harm than anything the earthquake might do.
- At home, keep a first-aid kit, a flashlight or lantern, a battery-powered radio, and a supply of batteries handy. Be sure everyone in your household knows where these items are stored.
- Learn first aid.
- Fasten heavy furniture securely to the floor and attach bookcases (or anything else that might topple over onto someone) firmly to the walls.
- Store heavy objects on low shelves, where they cannot hurt anyone if they fall.

• Memorize the locations of your electrical fuse box and the shut-off valves for gas and water. Everyone in your household should know how to turn them on and off.

• Arrange for household members to meet in a certain place, such as the backyard, in the event of an earthquake. This will help prevent anyone from getting lost.

Glossary

ACCELERATION. A measure of ground motion in an earthquake. Acceleration is defined as the time rate of change of velocity of a reference point during a quake. *See* G.

ACCELEROMETER. An instrument for measuring acceleration.

ACTIVE FAULT. Any fault that is seen as likely to generate earthquakes in the foreseeable future.

AFTERSHOCK. A weaker earthquake following a major one.

ALLUVIUM. In a general sense, loosely compacted sediment deposited by moving water. The Mississippi Delta is a famous example of an alluvial deposit.

AMPLIFICATION. An increase in amplitude of S-waves as the waves pass through a different earth material. *See* AMPLITUDE.

AMPLITUDE. A measure of earthquake intensity, equal to half the distance between the crest and trough of an earthquake wave.

ANTICLINE. An upwardly convex fold in initially level sedimentary rocks. In common usage, a hill or ridge produced by folding. *See* SYNCLINE.

AQUIFER. Water-bearing porous rock or sediment.

ASTHENOSPHERE. The layer of the earth immediately below the crust. *See* CRUST.

ATTENUATION. A decrease in amplitude in earthquake waves as they spread out from their source. *See* AMPLITUDE.

BASALT. A black, fine-grained volcanic rock.

BATHOLITH. A massive, deeply buried body of granitic rock like that found in the roots of the Sierra Nevada.

BEDROCK. Relatively hard, solid rock underlying softer sediment or soil.

BILLION. The billion used in this book is the American billion, or one followed by nine zeroes.

CENOZOIC. The current age of life on earth, also known as the age of mammals.

COHESION. The degree of internal bonding between particles in soil or sediment. In plain language, how well soil holds together in an earthquake.

COMPRESSIONAL FEATURES. Response of crustal plates to compression. *See* FOLDING, THRUSTING, TRENCHING, *and* THICKENING.

COMPUTER-ASSISTED TOMOGRAPHY. A process in which earthquake data are processed by computer to produce a three-dimensional image of density gradients inside the mantle. *See* MANTLE.

CONTINENTS. Major portions of the earth's crust projecting above sea level.

CORE. The dense innermost portion of the earth.

CRUST. The outer layer of the earth, in and just under which most earthquake activity takes place.

DAMPING. Reduction in amplitude of earthquake waves by energy absorption within a material. A "cushioning" effect, in other words. *See* AMPLITUDE, ATTENUATION.

DISPLACEMENT. How far something is moved from its initial place by an earthquake.

DOWN-DROPPING. The settling of crustal blocks in areas of tension. *See* TENSION.

EARTHQUAKE. Broadly defined, any periodic motion of the surface of the earth; more specifically, any measurable seismic activity. *See* SEISMICITY.

EPICENTER. The point on the earth's surface directly above the focus of an earthquake. *See* FOCUS.

EROSION. The gradual wearing away of surface rock by the action of wind, water, and ice.

FAULT. A crack or fissure separating blocks of crust; in common usage, an earthquake zone.

FISSURE. A crack in the earth's surface, commonly produced by earthquakes. Fissures vary greatly in length, depth, and width; some may extend more than a mile.

FOCUS. The point from which earthquake waves originate. The focus is usually some miles underground.

FOLDING. The pattern formed where compression squeezes the crust into a wavy pattern without thrusting or trenching. *See* THRUSTING, TRENCHING.

FORESHOCK. A relatively minor earthquake immediately preceding a major one.

FOSSILS. Remains of ancient life preserved, intact or as impressions, in rock.

FREQUENCY. A measure of vibration in cycles per second, or hertz (Hz).

FUNDAMENTAL FREQUENCY. The longest period for which a building or other structure shows a maximum response. In a sense, fundamental frequency is the number of cycles per second where a building vibrates "in tune" with an earthquake. *See* RESPONSE.

G. A unit of measurement of acceleration in an earthquake. G is better known as the gravitational constant, or the normal force of gravity at sea level, 980 centimeters (approximately 32 feet) per second per second. (That repeat of "per second" is not a typographical error; it is needed to make equations balance when the gravitational constant is used.) Ground motion in a typical moderate earthquake may be approximately .1 g, but measurements of 1.0 and higher are not unknown in major quakes. Ground motion of .2 g or higher suffices to destroy many buildings.

GONDWANA. The large southern fragment of the ancient supercontinent Pangaea. Gondwana, generally speaking, became the continents of today's Southern Hemisphere. *See* LAURUSSIA, PANGAEA.

HYDROCARBONS. Molecules consisting of chains of carbon atoms with hydrogen atoms attached. Petroleum is mostly hydrocarbons.

IGNEOUS ROCKS. Rocks formed directly by the cooling of molten rock. Granite is an example of an igneous rock.

ISOSTASY. The equilibrium attained by blocks of crustal rock "floating" on denser rock below.

LAURUSSIA. The large northern fragment of the ancient supercontinent Pangaea immediately after its breakup began. Generally speaking, Laurussia became the continents of today's Northern Hemisphere. *See* PANGAEA.

LAVA. Magma after it has emerged from underground onto the earth's surface. *See* MAGMA.

LIQUEFACTION. The process in which moist, unconsolidated material underground temporarily behaves as a liquid when subjected to shear from earthquake vibrations. *See* SHEAR.

MAGMA. Molten rock still underground.

MANTLE. The intermediate layer of the earth between the core and crust. *See* CORE, CRUST.

MESOZOIC. The intermediate age of life on earth, between the Paleozoic and the Cenozoic, in which we live. The Mesozoic was the heyday of the dinosaurs and is commonly known as the age of reptiles. *See* CENOZOIC, PALEOZOIC.

METAMORPHIC ROCK. Rock—usually sedimentary in origin— that has been transformed by subterranean heat and pressure into another form. Marble, for example, is a metamorphic form of limestone.

METHANE. A simple hydrocarbon molecule consisting of one carbon atom surrounded by four hydrogen atoms. Methane is better known as "marsh gas" or "swamp gas." *See* HYDROCARBONS.

MIDOCEAN RIDGES. Zones or "seams" in the earth's crust where magma solidifies to form new crust. *See* CRUST, MAGMA.

MILLION. The million used in this book is the American million, or one followed by six zeroes.

OUTGASSING. Release of gases from the earth's interior.

P-WAVES. Earthquake waves passing deep into the earth. Sometimes called "pressure waves."

PALEOZOIC. The earliest age of life on earth. Paleozoic life consisted mainly of marine species.

PANGAEA. The postulated ancient supercontinent of which the modern continents are believed to be fragments. *See* CONTINENTS.

PLATE TECTONICS. The theory that describes interactions among crustal plates. *See* CRUST, TECTONICS.

PRECAMBRIAN. In common usage, the period before life began on our planet. This usage is not quite accurate, however, because some very primitive organisms do appear to have lived during the Precambrian period.

RESPONSE. Anything an earthquake does to anything else. In ordinary usage, response means a building's reaction to quake vibrations.

RIFTING. The simple pulling apart of crustal blocks in areas of tension. *See* TENSION.

S-WAVES. Shear waves from an earthquake. *See* SHEAR.

SAND BLOW. Sand and water ejected from the earth's surface as a result of liquefaction underground. *See* LIQUEFACTION.

SATURATION. How much water soil, sediment, or rock contains.

SCARP. A steep vertical gradient produced by an earthquake or other geological process. In everyday language, a cliff made by an earthquake. Some scarps are more than one thousand feet high.

SCHIST. A common metamorphic rock.

SEDIMENT. Unconsolidated, eroded material deposited by wind and water.

SEDIMENTARY ROCK. Rock originally composed of sediment. Sandstone is a familiar example of sedimentary rock.

SEISMICITY. Generally speaking, earthquake activity or earthquake potential; short-term instability of the earth's crust not directly related to long-term processes such as erosion.

SEISMOGENIC. Capable of causing earthquakes.

SEISMOLOGY. The science of earthquakes.

SEISMOMETER. A device for detecting earthquakes.

SEISMOGRAPH. An earthquake-recording instrument.

SEISMOGRAM. A graphic record of earthquake vibrations.

SHEAR. In everyday terms, landslide potential, or a building's proneness to shift position during an earthquake. Technically, shear means motion at right angles to the direction of motion. *See* S-WAVES.

SILICATE. A rock bearing silicon dioxide.

STRIKE-SLIP FAULT. A fault along which motion is principally horizontal, with little or no vertical motion.

SUBDUCTION ZONES. Areas where crustal plates collide and are pushed down into the mantle. These areas are often characterized by deep ocean trenches.

SYNCLINE. A valley or other depression produced by folding. *See* ANTICLINE.

TECTONICS. The study of the large-scale features of the earth's surface and how they originated. In another sense, tectonics is the study of how the earth's surface rearranges itself.

TENSION. The pulling apart of crustal sections; the opposite of compression. *See* COMPRESSION.

TENSIONAL FEATURES. Response of crustal plates to tension. *See* TENSION. *Also* DOWN-DROPPING, RIFTING, *and* THINNING.

THICKENING. Increase in thickness of the crust where it is compressed.

THINNING. A decrease in crustal thickness caused by tension.

THRUSTING. The process in which blocks of crust are forced up and over one another, in a pattern much like fallen dominoes, where two crustal plates meet head on.

THRUST FAULT. A fault where thrusting takes place.

TRACE. Intersection of a fault with the surface. Also, the line on a geologic map indicating where a fault runs.

TRENCHING. The process of trench formation where two crustal plates collide and one is subducted under the other. *See* SUBDUCTION ZONES.

TSUNAMI. A seismic sea wave produced by an earthquake, volcanic eruption, or other geophysical disturbance. Tsunamis are commonly but inaccurately known as "tidal waves."

TSUNAMIGENIC. Capable of causing tsunamis. *See* TSUNAMI.

VOLCANO. A single point where magma emerges from underground onto the earth's surface; also, a mountain formed by this process.

VULCANISM. Volcanic activity. *See* VOLCANO.

WAVELENGTH. Distance from one wave crest to another.

Further Reading

Since this is not a work of scholarship, a formal bibliography is not needed. Here instead is a brief list of source material.

Earthquakes and Seismology

The popular literature on seismology is huge and constantly growing. For an entertaining overview of quake science, see the Leets' little paperback, *Earthquake: Discoveries in Seismology* (New York: Dell, 1964). Robert Iacopi's *Earthquake Country* provides a good introduction to California earthquakes and is liberally illustrated with dramatic photos. Preston Cloud's *Adventures in Earth Science* (San Francisco: Freeman, 1970), while technical in places, is nonetheless recommended. The genesis of plate tectonics is outlined in Walter Sullivan's classic *Continents in Motion* (New York: McGraw-Hill, 1974) and Ursula Marvin's *Continental Drift: The Evolution of a Concept* (Washington, D.C.: Smithsonian Institution, 1973). Alfred Wegener's own book, *The Origins of the Oceans and Continents*, is available in English translation (New York: Methuen, 1967). Haroun Tazieff's little volume, *When the Earth Trembles* (New York: Harcourt Brace and World, 1964), is a colorful and nontechnical introduction to earthquake science, though it was written before the theory of plate tectonics came to be widely accepted. For a more up-to-date treatment, see Peter Verney's *The Earthquake Handbook* (London: Paddington, 1979), Bruce Bolt's *Earthquakes: A Primer* (New York: Freeman, 1978), and the Bird and Isaacs anthology, *Plate Tectonics: Selected Papers from the Journal of Geophysical Research* (Washington, D.C.: American Geophysical Union, 1972). Readers with patience and a firm background in the physical sciences may want to read a survey of seismology by Charles Richter, one of the luminaries in that field: *Elementary Seismology* (San Fransicso: Freeman, 1958).

California's Quake Potential

California geology, with emphasis on earthquakes, is the subject of Oakeshott's excellent volume, *California's Changing Landscapes* (New York: McGraw-Hill, 1978). For a look at how Californians living along the San Andreas Fault view their precarious situation, read the article by Raymond Sullivan et al, "Living in Earthquake Country: A Survey of Residents Living Along the San Andreas Fault," *Calfornia Geology*, January 1977, pp. 3–8.

The federal government's study of quake potential in southern California is summarized in a small pamphlet entitled *An Assessment of the Consequences and Preparations for a Catastrophic California Earthquake: Findings and Actions Taken* (Washington, D.C.: Federal Emergency Management Agency, 1980). The title may be dry, but the information in the pamphlet is sobering. Read it for an understanding of how little we know about the consequences of superquakes in modern cities.

The San Fernando Earthquake

The 1971 San Fernando earthquake is the subject of two brief but informative reports. One is *The San Fernando, California, Earthquake of February 9, 1971: Geological Survey Professional Paper 733* (Washington, D.C.: U.S. Government Printing Office, 1971). This is a comprehensive and well-illustrated study covering all scientific aspects of the earthquake. When ordering this report, be sure to ask specifically for professional paper 733; the number will allow the government to process your order faster. The second report, which deals mainly with damage to buildings, is *The San Fernando Earthquake, February 9, 1971* (San Francisco: Pacific Fire Rating Bureau, 1971).

For an exhaustive scientific study of the San Fernando quake, including a discussion of its implications for future earthquakes in southern California, see U.S. Geological Survey Paper 1360, *Evaluating Earthquake Hazards in the Los Angeles Region—An Earth-Science Perspective* (Washington, D.C.: U.S. Government Printing Office, 1985). Of special interest is the next-to-last chapter, concerning the predicted effects of a postulated major earthquake in the L.A. area.

The San Fernando earthquake is recounted in Peter Briggs's book *Will California Fall into the Sea?* (New York: McKay, 1972).

The New Madrid Earthquakes

Readers already versed in geology may wish to consult the U.S. Geological Survey's study of quake hazards in the Midwest, *Estimation of Earthquake Effects Associated with Large Earthquakes in the New Madrid Seismic Zone, Open-File Report 85-457* (Washington, D.C.: U.S. Geological Survey, 1985). This slim volume contains, among other things, a history of quake activity in the Mississippi River valley and an excellent set of maps showing how the consequences of a major earthquake there could upset the entire Midwest. An entertaining history of the New Madrid disaster is James Lal Penick's little paperback, *The New Madrid, Missouri, Earthquakes* (St. Louis: University of Missouri Press, 1980). Penick's work is a rarity—a sound, scholarly history that keeps the reader turning pages. His study of the psychology of quake survivors is both amusing and enlightening and helps illuminate the motives and methods of demagogues and fear-mongers in our own time. Penick's comments on the New Madrid earthquakes and the history of the Native Americans are especially poignant and revealing.

The San Francisco Earthquake

San Francisco's 1906 earthquake is the subject of thousands of books and articles. Perhaps the best single history of the disaster written for nonscientists is *The Great San Francisco Earthquake* (New York: Stein and Day, 1971), by Gordon Thomas and Max Witts. Harder to find, but entertaining, is Thom Willenbecher's essay on how Californians live with the threat of seismic destruction, "The Quake As an Article of Faith in California," *Baltimore Sun*, July 20, 1980, p. K3.

The Deep Gas Hypothesis

The deep gas hypothesis is explained in several articles for popular journals. See "The Origin of Petroleum" by David Osborne, *The Atlantic*, February 1986; "Afloat on a Sea of Methane?" *Technology Review*, October 1978, pp. 14–15; "Methane from the Bowels of the Earth," *New Scientist*, June 29, 1978, pp. 896–897; and "Right or Wrong, Thomas Gold Is Proving Provocative Again," *New York Times*, October 7, 1980, p. C1. These articles are especially interesting because they show how scientists may draw dramatically different conclusions from the same body of data.

Tsunamis

Tsunamis are a fascinating study, and readers interested in them may enjoy Franklin Smith's book *The Seas in Motion* (New York: Crowell, 1973). See also Keith Hindley's article, "Beware the Big Wave," *New Scientist*, February 9, 1978, pp. 346–347. A more scholarly treatment of tsunamis may be found in D. S. McCullough's essay, "Evaluating Tsunami Potential," in U.S. Geological Survey Professional Paper 1360 (see above). Recommended scientific works on tsunamis include "Damage Survey of the Nihon-Kai-Chubu, Japan, Earthquake of May 26, 1983," by V. V. Bertero et al, *Earthquake Spectra*, vol. 1, no. 2 (1985), pp. 319–352; "Tsunami History of San Diego," by D. C. Agnew, in *Earthquakes and Other Perils, San Diego Region* (San Diego, CA: San Diego Association of Geologists, 1983), pp. 117–122; and the Coulter and Migliacco report on the effects of the Alaskan Good Friday earthquake of 1964, in U.S. Geological Survey Professional Paper 542-C (Washington, D.C.: U.S. Government Printing Office, 1966), pp. C1–C36.

Notes

Chapter 1

Page 9. "a fissure 'a hundred feet long' ": One popular image of earthquakes is that of the "man-eating" fissure, a great crack that supposedly opens in the ground, swallows anyone unfortunate enough to be standing above, and then closes again, crushing the victim to death. This is a misconception. There is no documented instance of anyone ever being killed in this manner. The myth of killer fissures may have originated with the writings of Navy Lieutenant J. G. Billings, who was on the USS *Wateree* when the ship was caught in a tsunami at the port of Arica, Peru, in 1868. The *Wateree* survived the great wave, and as its crew afterward explored the devastation on shore, the sailors found a grisly sight: the body of a woman seated on a dead horse, "both having been swallowed by [the] crevasse as they were flying for their lives." Billings did not say specifically that the woman and horse had been pressed to death by the fissure as it closed; more likely they merely fell into the opening and were killed, or they died elsewhere and were dumped there pending proper burial. There was another alleged instance of a fissure opening and killing a cow, during the San Francisco earthquake of 1906, but later it was revealed that the animal had died upon falling into the fissure, and passersby had buried it there, giving the impression that the crack had sealed itself and crushed the cow.

Page 13. "perfectly mad people": Among the maddest of all San Franciscans in the nineteenth century was Joshua Abraham Norton, the self-styled "Emperor of the United States and Protector of Mexico." Norton was a South African businessman who went insane after one of his ventures failed and proclaimed himself the Emperor Norton I. A portly man with mustache and goatee, he wore an elaborate uniform and paraded around San Francisco in the company of his two dogs, who went with him everywhere—even to the opera, where they shared box seats with him. Norton had no job; he supported himself by issuing notes decorated with his likeness and drawn on the nonexistent "imperial treasury of Norton I." Banks and shops honored them. Humored by the tolerant San Franciscans, Norton lived in reasonable comfort, if not luxury, and became something of a social lion. When one of his dogs died, half the city, including its civic leaders, showed up for the funeral. Nothing intimidated Emperor Norton, who once crashed a reception for the viceroy of Mexico, saying, "I am his equal, and possibly greater!" Norton sometimes is given credit for originating the design for the modern suspension bridge. Whether or not he really did so, he was among the first to propose building bridges where the Golden Gate Bridge and the Bay Bridge to Oakland stand today.

Page 17. "Caruso was acquitted of this canard": Among the other historical figures cleared of unbecoming conduct by the San Francisco court is Marshal Wyatt Earp, a gunslinger of shady reputation. The Court of Historical Appeals ruled that Earp actually had shown high moral character by the lenient standards of his day.

Page 18. "Jack London, best-selling author": London survived the San Francisco earthquake, several wars, and all manner of other perils on sea and land in his forty-odd years of life. London the man was a fascinating study in paradoxes. He called himself a "materialist monist," meaning one who does not believe in the duality of body and spirit; yet his novel *The Star Rover* amounted to a vivid defense of spiritualism. London is recognized as an expert on prospecting and on the Arctic, but he spent only a few weeks in the far north and was notably unsuccessful in finding gold. And though he called himself a socialist and said he hated the rich and wanted economic equality for all, he became a millionaire from his writings, many of which espoused a Social Darwinist philosophy. Toward the end of his life, seeing that socialism seemed unworkable, he abandoned it and devoted himself largely to the management of his California ranch. It is widely believed that London committed suicide, since the hero of his autobiographical novel *Martin Eden* kills himself by drowning at the end of the story; but in fact London died from a renal disorder. One interesting sidelight on his career is that he anticipated by more than half a century the current Soviet practice of sending political dissidents to mental institutions. In his novel *The Iron Heel*, a future totalitarian state uses this same maneuver to get rid of an activist clergyman. Among the best introductions to London and his work is Russ Kingman's *Jack London: An Illustrated Biography* (New York: Crown, 1982).

Chapter 2

Page 47. "a spongy-textured earth": Hollow-earth theories had influential adherents until well into the twentieth century. German Chancellor Adolf Hitler reportedly sent a flotilla of warships on a bizarre mission to conduct geodetic measurements aimed at proving or disproving a hollow-earth hypothesis.

Page 47. *"Journey to the Center of the Earth"*: Verne's novel was made into an implausible but entertaining motion picture starring James Mason. Not all Verne's books were such innocent good fun; his outer-space fantasy *Hector Servadac (Off on a Comet),* for example, was marred by an ugly streak of anti-Semitism.

Page 51. *"diluvianism"*: This odd, Bible-based school of thought is far from dead today. Biblical literalists even urge that it be taught as legitimate science in public schools.

Page 54. "Ignatius Donnelly": A Minnesotan, Donnelly is remembered primarily for his career in politics (he ran for president as the Populist candidate in 1900, on a ticket so radical that newspapers dubbed it the "platform of lunacy"), but he also went down in history for some of his nonpolitical convictions. Besides his views on the history of Atlantis, he believed that the plays of William Shakespeare contained a code that proved Francis Bacon had actually written them. Donnelly also created a sensation by proposing, in his 1882 novel *Ragnarok,* that many great natural disasters in human history were caused by a colossal comet that passed close to the earth in ancient times. Donnelly's lurid descriptions of the fictional comet aside, *Ragnarok* was little more than a Populist political tract; the story closed with a sermon on the need to redistribute wealth from the rich to the poor. The furor caused by Donnelly's book was still fresh in the public's mind when Halley's comet returned in 1910, and the panic that accompanied the comet's passage probably owed much to Donnelly's bizarre visions. For an entertaining account of Donnelly's career as a novelist, see Martin Gardner's book *Fads and Fallacies in the Name of Science* (New York: Dover, 1952).

Page 55. "some one hundred million years ago": The currently accepted figure is closer to 180 million years ago. Pangaea is believed to have started breaking up about the time the first dinosaurs appeared on earth.

Chapter 9

Page 133. "the folklore of New England": Earthquakes have had less impact on New England literature, but Oliver Wendell Holmes used an earthquake to poke fun at the ultralogical Yankee clergymen of his time, in his poem "The Deacon's Masterpiece; or, the Wonderful One-Hoss Shay." In the poem a deacon ponders why his buggy keeps needing repairs. Logic leads him to conclude that one part or another is weaker than the rest and therefore more prone to failure. His solution is to build a buggy whose every component is as strong as every other. Then, he figures, the vehicle should keep running indefinitely without needing repairs. He builds such a buggy, only to see every last part of it shaken to bits at once when an earthquake hits. Holmes's message is that there are limits to the utility of logic. As Holmes puts it in the final stanza:

> *End of the wonderful one-hoss shay.*
> *Logic is logic. That's all I say.*

Page 139. "hundreds of old trees": Observers of the New Madrid quakes were especially puzzled to see ancient trees rising from the deep to the surface. This effect was later explained in terms of sedimentation, or the deposition of mud and silt by the river. Supposedly the logs had been buried by a rapid accumulation of sediment while some buoyancy remained in them; when the earthquake released the trees from the grip of the muck that held them, they proceeded to float back to the surface.

Page 143. "great terror": Then as now, earthquakes held an eschatological significance for conservative Christians, who interpret the Bible to say that the expected return of Christ will be preceded by great earthquakes in various corners of the world. Other alleged signs of Christ's impending return include punk rock, the Iranian revolution, and the rise to power of Libyan strongman Muammar Qaddafi.

Page 145. "The 1840 election": This campaign was dirty even by twentieth-century standards. Van Buren's supporters tried to portray Harrison as a rustic drunkard who lived in a log cabin and swilled hard cider. Harrison's campaigners turned this slur to their advantage, however, by packaging their man as the "hard cider candidate," a humble and rugged soul, as opposed to the elegant and effete Van Buren. Here is a stanza from a Harrison campaign song:

> *Let Van from his goblets of silver drink wine*
> *And lounge on his cushioned settee;*
> *Our man on a hardwood bench can recline,*
> *Content with hard cider is he!*

Index